Knitting
with your **leftovers**

Knitting
with your **leftovers**

25 GREAT WAYS TO USE UP YOUR YARN LEFTOVERS OF ONE BALL OR LESS

FIONA GOBLE

CICO BOOKS
LONDON NEW YORK

Published in 2020 by CICO Books
An imprint of Ryland Peters & Small Ltd
20–21 Jockey's Fields   341 E 116th St
London WC1R 4BW   New York, NY 10029

www.rylandpeters.com

10 9 8 7 6 5 4 3 2

Text © Fiona Goble 2020
Design, illustration, and photography © CICO Books 2020

Patterns in this book have previously appeared in one of
the following titles by Fiona Goble: *Cute and Easy Knitting*;
Knitted Animal Nursery.

A CIP catalog record for this book is available from the
Library of Congress and the British Library.

ISBN: 978 1 78249 900 8

Printed in China

Editor: Marie Clayton
Photographers: Caroline Arber and Terry Benson
Stylists: Nel Haynes, Sophie Martell, and Rob Merrett
Illustrator: Stephen Dew

In-house designer: Eliana Holder
Art director: Sally Powell
Head of production: Patricia Harrington
Publishing manager: Penny Craig
Publisher: Cindy Richards

Contents

Introduction 6

Introduction

If you're a big knitting fan, you'll know how it happens. You've got a ball left over from this project… a half-ball left over from that project…. And in no time at all, you've got a big bag or a box (or in my case quite a large closet) overflowing with odd balls of yarn. You don't want to give them away—you love them too much—but you can't think exactly what to do with your precious knitting stash.

That's where this book comes to the rescue, with a collection of patterns that use a maximum of one ball of each type or shade of yarn. I have included details of the yarn I used for the original pattern, but so long as the yarn you use knits up to the same gauge (tension), you should be absolutely fine, even if the finished result has a slightly different look. (For more information on substituting yarn, visit yarnsub.com, and also see page 81.)

I've divided the book into three sections. There are projects for the home, including my personal favorite, the Owl Storage Baskets (page 14). And there are things to knit for baby—you're going to find it hard to resist those cute Rabbit Bootees (page 46). Finally there's a section I've called Bits and Bobs, with patterns to create a range of quirky objects, including some fabulous heart bunting (page 62).

Most of the projects are suitable for adventurous beginners and some even for knitting newbies, but before you begin, have a look through the pattern to make sure everything's clear. The Techniques section (pages 80–94) includes instructions for anything you are not familiar with.

For me, one of the best things about knitting is that with a bit of confidence and experimentation, it's so easy to add your own touches to a basic pattern and get fabulous results. You can simply change a color or use a yarn with a different look. So please, check out your stash, soak in some inspiration—and create something to fall in love with.

Fiona Goble
fionagoble.com

CHAPTER 1
For the Home

Cottage Doorstop

Why use an ordinary old doorstop when you can knit yourself a pretty little cottage? Knitted in two strands of light worsted (DK) yarn, the cottage comes together much quicker than you'd think. We've chosen to knit our cottage in cream—but it would also work well in white, pale yellow, or pastel pink.

YARN AND OTHER MATERIALS

Patons Diploma Gold DK (55% wool, 25% acrylic, 20% nylon; 131yd/120m per 1¾oz/50g ball) light worsted (DK) yarn
   1 ball of shade 6142 Cream (A)

Sublime Baby Cashmere Merino Silk DK (75% merino wool, 20% silk, 5% cashmere; 127yd/116m per 1¾oz/50g ball) light worsted (DK) yarn
   1 ball of shade 277 Tittlemouse (B) (dark gray)

Debbie Bliss Rialto DK (100% merino wool; 115yd/105m per 1¾oz/50g ball) light worsted (DK) yarn
   Small amount of shade 12 Scarlet (C)
   Small amount of shade 09 Apple (D) (green)

For the variation
Small amounts of light worsted (DK) yarns in shades:
   Light turquoise (E)
   Yellow (F)

3–4 small decorative buttons

Approx. 2½ cups (8oz/500g) uncooked rice or dried lentils

Medium size polythene bag

Approx. 2oz (50g) 100% polyester toy filling

NEEDLES AND EQUIPMENT

Size US 8 (5mm) knitting needles

Size US 2/3 (3mm) knitting needles (for variation)

Yarn sewing needle

Large-eyed embroidery needle

Water-erasable pen

GAUGE (TENSION)

18 sts and 26 rows in stockinette (stocking) stitch to a 4-in (10-cm) square on US 8 (5mm) needles, using yarn double.

MEASUREMENTS

The doorstop is 6½in (16.5cm) high.

ABBREVIATIONS

approx.	approximately
beg	begin(ning)
k	knit
k2tog	knit two stitches together
kwise	knitwise
p	purl
ssk	slip one stitch, slip one stitch, knit slipped stitches together
st(s)	stitch(es)
st st	stockinette (stocking) stitch

Cottage

FRONT/BACK PANEL

(make 2 the same)
Cast on 22 sts in A, using yarn double.
Work 14 rows in st st beg with a k row.
Row 15: K1, k2tog, k to last 3 sts, ssk, k1. (*20 sts*)
Work 9 rows in st st beg with a p row.
Row 25: K1, k2tog, k to last 3 sts, ssk, k1. (*18 sts*)
Row 26: P.
Fasten off A and join double strand of B.
K 2 rows.
Work 2 rows in st st beg with a k row.
K 2 rows.
Rep last 4 rows once more.
Row 37: K1, k2tog, k to last 3 sts, ssk, k1. (*16 sts*)
Row 38: P.
K 2 rows.
Bind (cast) off.

SIDE PANEL

(make 2 the same)
Cast on 16 sts in A, using yarn double.
Work 14 rows in st st beg with a k row.
Row 15: K1, k2tog, k to last 3 sts, ssk, k1. (*14 sts*)
Work 9 rows in st st beg with a p row.
Row 25: K1, k2tog, k to last 3 sts, ssk, k1. (*12 sts*)
Row 26: P.
Fasten off A and join double strand of B.
K 2 rows.
Work 2 rows in st st beg with a k row.
K 2 rows.
Rep last 4 rows once more.
Row 37: K1, k2tog, k to last 3 sts, ssk, k1. (*10 sts*)
Row 38: P.
K 2 rows.
Bind (cast) off.

BASE

(make 1)
Cast on 22 sts in A, using yarn double.
Work 20 rows in st st beg with a k row.
Bind (cast) off.

TOP

(make 1)
Cast on 16 sts in B, using yarn double.
Work 12 rows in st st beg with a k row.
Bind (cast) off.

Strap

(make 1)
Cast on 4 sts in B, using yarn double.
K 22 rows.
Bind (cast) off.

Making up and finishing

Using A, sew one side panel to each side of one of the front/back panels with mattress stitch (see page 92). Sew the second front/back panel to the side panels, again using mattress stitch. From the inside, oversew (see page 91) the base in place along four sides and oversew two sides of the top in place.

Put the rice or dried lentils into the polythene bag and insert into the doorstop. Fill the remainder of the doorstop with fiberfill toy filling and stitch the remaining two sides of the top. Oversew the ends of the strap in place.

Mark the position of windows and door using the water-erasable pen. Using B, work the window frame and cross bars in straight stitch (see page 93). Using C, work the door outline in chain stitch (see page 93). Using D, work the stems of flowers in straight stitch. Stitch on buttons for the flowers.

Variation

Make up the cottage and strap as before, then knit the windows and door as follows:

WINDOWS
(make 2)
Cast on 7 sts in E.
Work 7 rows in st st beg with a k row.
Bind (cast) off.

DOOR
(make 1)
Cast on 8 sts in C.
Work 15 rows in st st beg with a k row.
Bind (cast) off kwise.

Making up and finishing

Oversew windows and doors in place using matching yarns.

Using B, work four straight stitches from the center of the window to the mid-point of each side. Using F, work the flowers in lazy daisy stitch (see page 93). Using B, work French knots (see page 93) for the flower centers. Using D, work each flower stem in straight stitch and each leaf in a single lazy daisy stitch.

Owl Storage Baskets

These handy storage baskets not only look lovely, they'll also keep all your bits and pieces tidily stashed away, ready for when you need them. The owls are knitted in a simple seed (moss) stitch to create an interesting texture, and although I've chosen a robust citrus shade for mine, you could use whatever color would complement your décor. Did I mention that the pattern includes baskets in two sizes?

YARN AND OTHER MATERIALS

Debbie Bliss Roma (70% wool, 30% alpaca; 87yd/80m per 3½oz/100g ball) super-bulky (super-chunky) yarn
 1 ball of shade 008 Citrus (A)

Small amounts of dark gray (B) and orange (C) light worsted (DK) yarns

Very small amount of off-white light worsted (DK) yarn

2 x ½-in (12-mm) pale blue buttons for larger basket

2 x ⁵⁄₁₆-in (8-mm) pale blue buttons for smaller basket

Black sewing thread

Very small amount of 100% polyester toy filling

NEEDLES AND EQUIPMENT

US 15 (10mm) knitting needles

US 7 (4.5mm) knitting needles

Yarn sewing needle

Large-eyed embroidery needle

Standard sewing needle

GAUGE (TENSION)

10 sts and 13 rows in stockinette (stocking) stitch to a 4-in (10-cm) square on US 15 (10mm) needles.

MEASUREMENTS

The finished larger basket stands 6½in (16.5cm) tall and the smaller one 3½in (9cm) tall.

ABBREVIATIONS

beg	begin(ning)
k	knit
k2tog	knit two stitches together
p	purl
p2tog	purl two stitches together
psso	pass slipped stitch(es) over
rem	remain(ing)
rep	repeat
sl1	slip one stitch from the left-hand needle to the right-hand needle without knitting it
ssk	slip one stitch, slip one stitch, knit slipped stitches together
st(s)	stitch(es)
st st	stockinette (stocking) stitch
[ ]	work instructions within square brackets as directed

Large basket

BODY

Using US 15 (10mm) needles, cast on 34 sts in A.
Beg with a k row, work 4 rows in st st.
Row 5: [K1, p1] to end.
Row 6: [P1, k1] to end.
Rep rows 5–6 twelve times more.
Row 31: [K2tog] to end. (*17 sts*)
Row 32: K.
Row 33: K1, [k2tog] to end. (*9 sts*)
Row 34: K.
Break yarn and thread through rem sts.

WINGS

(make 2)
Using US 15 (10mm) needles, cast on 5 sts in A.
Row 1: [K1, p1] to last st, k1.
Rep row 1 five times more.
Row 7: P2tog, k1, p2tog. (*3 sts*)
Row 8: P1, k1, p1.
Row 9: Sl1, k2tog, psso. (*1 st*)
Fasten off.

EYE BASES

(make 2)
Using US 7 (4.5mm) needles, cast on 20 sts in B, using yarn double.
Row 1: [K2tog] to end. (*10 sts*)
Row 2: [P2tog] to end. (*5 sts*)
Break yarn, thread through rem sts, and secure.

BEAK

Using US 7 (4.5mm) needles, cast on 8 sts in C, using yarn double.
Beg with a k row, work 2 rows in st st.
Row 3: K1, ssk, k2, k2tog, k1. (*6 sts*)
Row 4: P2tog, p2, p2tog. (*4 sts*)
Break yarn and thread through rem sts, and secure.

Small basket

BODY

Using US 15 (10mm) needles, cast on 22 sts in A.
Beg with a k row, work 4 rows in st st.
Row 5: [K1, p1] to end.
Row 6: [P1, k1] to end.
Rep rows 5–6 five times more.
Row 17: [K2tog] to end. (*11 sts*)
Row 18: K.
Row 19: K1, [k2tog] to end. (*6 sts*)
Row 20: K.
Break yarn and thread through rem sts.

WINGS

(make 2)
Using US 15 (10mm) needles, cast on 3 sts in A.
Row 1: K1, p1, k1.
Rep row 1 four times more.
Row 6: Sl1, k2tog, psso. (*1 st*)
Fasten off.

EYE BASES

(make 2)
Using US 7 (4.5mm) needles, cast on 16 sts in B, using
yarn double.
Row 1: [K2tog] to end. (*8 sts*)
Row 2: [P2tog] to end. (*4 sts*)
Break yarn, thread through rem sts, and secure.

BEAK

Using US 7 (4.5mm) needles, cast on 6 sts in C, using
yarn double.
Beg with a k row, work 2 rows in st st.
Row 3: K1, ssk, k2tog, k1. (*4 sts*)
Break yarn and thread through rem sts, and secure.

Making up and finishing

Join the lower and back seam of the basket using flat
stitch (see page 91).

Oversew (see page 91) the wings in position at the sides.

Oversew the eye bases in position. Using off-white yarn,
work 8-point stars on the eye bases of the larger basket
and 6-point stars on the eye bases of the smaller basket,
using the photograph as a guide. Sew the buttons in
place using black thread.

Sew the long seam of the beak, leaving the lower edge
open. Stuff very lightly and oversew the beak in place.

Weave in all loose ends.

Coat Hanger Covers

Why hang your favorite outfits on boring old coat hangers, when with a small amount of leftover yarn and a bit of imagination you can hang them on a coat hanger with its very own knitted cover? As well as looking gorgeous, these knitted covers will make sure your best dress does not slip off the hanger in your closet and become damaged!

YARN AND OTHER MATERIALS

For the striped cover
Debbie Bliss Rialto DK (100% merino wool; 115yd/105m per 1¾oz/50g ball) light worsted (DK) yarn
   1 ball of shade 76 Rose (A) (pink)
   1 part ball of shade 09 Apple (B) (green)

For the cable stitch cover
Debbie Bliss Rialto DK (100% merino wool; 115yd/105m per 1¾oz/50g ball) light worsted (DK) yarn
   1 ball of shade 54 Mint (C) (pale green)

NEEDLES AND EQUIPMENT

Size US 3 (3.25mm) knitting needles

Small or medium cable needle (for cable stitch cover)

Yarn sewing needle

2 x 17-in (43-cm) wooden coat hangers

GAUGE (TENSION)

20 sts and 48 rows in garter stitch and 25 sts and 36 rows in cable stitch pattern to a 4-in (10-cm) square on US 3 (3.25mm) needles.

MEASUREMENTS

To fit standard wooden coat hangers measuring 17in (43cm) across.

ABBREVIATIONS

approx.	approximately
C4F	cable four front
k	knit
p	purl
RS	right side(s)
st(s)	stitch(es)

Striped cover

COVER
(make 1)
Cast on 18 sts in A.
Rows 1–6: K.
Leave A at side and join in B.
Rows 7–8: K.
Rep last 8 rows 18 times more.
K 6 rows in A.
Bind (cast) off.

POMPOM TRIM
Make 2 pompoms in B (see page 94), each approx. 1¼in (3cm) in diameter. Braid (plait) three lengths of yarn to make a 4¾-in (12-cm) length of cord. Fasten a pompom to each end of the cord.

Cable stitch cover

(make 1)
Cast on 19 sts in C.
Row 1: P3, k4, p5, k4, p3.
Row 2: K3, p4, k5, p4, k3.
Row 3: P3, C4F, p5, C4F, p3.
Row 4: K3, p4, k5, p4, k3.
Rep last 4 rows 33 times more.
Bind (cast) off.

Making up and finishing

Fold the knitted strips in half lengthways with RS out and join one of the short ends and half of the long seam using mattress stitch (see page 92) and matching yarn.

Put the cover over the hanger, carefully taking the hook through a gap between stitches in your knitting.

Complete the long seam and the second short seam using mattress stitch. Wrap the pompom trim round the striped coat hanger.

Wash Cloths

These pretty wash cloths are knitted in a beautifully soft pure cotton yarn using a simple lacy stitch. They are an ideal first project if you're just learning to knit lace because there is no shaping or any fancy edges. Cotton yarns come in some beautiful colors, so knit a batch for your kitchen or bathroom and you will never want to use a boring old flannel again.

YARN AND OTHER MATERIALS

Rowan Cotton Glace (100% cotton; 125yd/115m per 1¾oz/50g ball) light worsted (DK) yarn

1 ball each of shades:
858 Aqua (A) (bright blue)
814 Shoot (B) (green)

NEEDLES AND EQUIPMENT

Size US 5 (3.75mm) knitting needles

Yarn sewing needle

GAUGE (TENSION)

19 sts and 25 rows in lace pattern to a 4-in (10-cm) square on US 5 (3.75mm) needles.

MEASUREMENTS

Each wash cloth measures approx. 11in (28cm) square.

ABBREVIATIONS

approx.	approximately
k	knit
k2tog	knit two stitches together
p	purl
psso	pass slipped stitch over, pass a slipped stitch over another stitch
rep	repeat
sl1	slip one stitch from the left-hand needle to the right-hand needle without knitting it
st(s)	stitch(es)
yo	yarnover
[ ]	work instructions within square brackets as directed

Cloth

(make 1 in A and 1 in B)
Cast on 57 sts in either A or B.
K 4 rows.
Row 5: K5, [yo, sl1, k2tog, psso, yo, k1] to last 4 sts, k4.
Row 6: K3, p to last 3 sts, k3.
Row 7: K4, k2tog, yo, k1 [yo, sl1, k2tog, psso, yo, k1] to last 6 sts, yo, sl1, k1, psso, k4.
Row 8: K3, p to last 3 sts, k3.
Rep last 4 rows 15 times more.
K 4 rows.
Bind (cast) off.

Making up and finishing

Weave in all loose ends.

YARN AND OTHER MATERIALS

Schachenmayr Merino Extrafine 120
(100% wool; 131yd/120m per 1¾oz/50g
ball) light worsted (DK) yarn
  Part ball each of shades:
  175 Limone (pale green)
  145 Flieder (pale mauve)

NEEDLES AND EQUIPMENT

Size US 2/3 (3mm) knitting needles
Size US 7 (4.5mm) crochet hook
Yarn sewing needle
Small safety pin to thread the cord

GAUGE (TENSION)

21 sts and 27 rows in pattern for main
section to a 4-in (10-cm) square on
US 2/3 (3mm) needles.

MEASUREMENTS

The cover measures approx. 6¼in
(16cm) and will fit a jar top approx. 3½in
(9cm) in diameter.

ABBREVIATIONS

approx.	approximately
k	knit
k2tog	knit two stitches together
psso	pass slipped stitch(es) over
p	purl
pwise	purlwise
rem	remain(ing)
rep	repeat
RH	right-hand
RS	right side(s)
sl1	slip one stitch from the left-hand needle to the right-hand needle without knitting it
st(s)	stitch(es)
yo	yarnover
[ ]	work instructions within square brackets as directed

Jam Jar Cover

Don't put up with dreary jam jars a moment longer! This
delicate cover will bring a spark of vintage cheer to any
kitchen storage jar—or use it in the bathroom on a jar that
stores soaps or cosmetics. It's knitted in two types of easy-to-
work lace and finished off with a co-ordinating cord made from
a simple crochet chain. It really doesn't matter if the cover
comes out a little larger or smaller, so why not try out a pretty
yarn that matches the color of your kitchen or your crockery.

Cover

MAIN COVER
Cast on 27 sts in A.
Row 1 (RS): K2 [yo, sl1, k2tog, psso, yo, k1] to last st, k1.
Row 2: P.
Row 3: K1, k2tog, yo, k1, [yo, sl1, k2tog, psso, yo, k1] to last 3 sts, yo, sl1, k1, psso, k1.
Row 4: P.
Rep last 4 rows 9 times more.
Bind (cast) off pwise.

LACE TRIM
The trim is made separately.
Cast on 7 sts in A.
Row 1: K1, [k2tog, yo twice] twice, k2. (*9 sts*)
Row 2: K3, [p1, k2] twice.
Row 3: K1, k2tog, yo twice, k2tog, k4.
Row 4: Bind (cast) off 2 sts (1 st rem on RH needle), k3, p1, k2. (*7 sts*)
Rep last 4 rows 32 times more.
Bind (cast) off.

Cord

Using B double, make a 28-in (70-cm) crochet chain (see page 94).

Making up and finishing

Oversew the lace trim to the outer edges of the main cover. Join cast-on and bound-(cast-) off edges.

Weave the yarn tails at each end of the cord back into itself. Using the small safety pin, thread the cord in and out of the lace pattern, starting at the center of one side, and using the photographs below as a guide.

Mug Cozy

Keep your drinks warmer for longer by knitting a cozy for your favorite mug. This is an ideal project if you're just learning how to work cable stitches—so impressive and so much easier than they look. We finished our cozy off with a little strap that slots through the handle, but you could leave it unadorned if you don't have enough yarn; it'll look great either way.

YARN AND OTHER MATERIALS

Schachenmayr Merino Extrafine 120 (100% wool; 131yd/120m per 1¾oz/50g ball) light worsted (DK) yarn
  1 ball of shade 173 Apfel (green)

1 x ¾-in (18-mm) pale blue button

Standard white sewing thread

NEEDLES AND EQUIPMENT

Size US 8 (5mm) knitting needles

Medium cable needle

Yarn sewing needle

Standard sewing needle

GAUGE (TENSION)

20 sts and 26 rows in stockinette (stocking) stitch to a 4-in (10-cm) square on US 8 (5mm) needles, using yarn double.

MEASUREMENTS

To fit an average size mug (12fl oz/ 360ml) with straight sides.

ABBREVIATIONS

C6B   cable six back
C6F   cable six front
k   knit
p   purl
rep   repeat
st(s)   stitch(es)

Cozy

(make 1)
Cast on 17 sts, using yarn double.
K 2 rows.
Row 3: K1, p3, k9, p3, k1.
Row 4: K4, p9, k4.
Rep last 2 rows 3 times more.
Row 11: K1, p3, k3, C6F, p3, k1.
Row 12: K4, p9, k4.
Row 13: K1, p3, k9, p3, k1.
Row 14: K4, p9, k4.
Row 15: K1, p3, C6B, k3, p3, k1.
Row 16: K4, p9, k4.
Row 17: K1, p3, k9, p3, k1.
Row 18: K4, p9, k4.
Rep rows 11–18 five times more.
K 3 rows.
Bind (cast) off.

Handle strap

(make 1)
Cast on 7 sts, using yarn double.
K 6 rows.
Row 7: K3, bind (cast) off 2 sts, K to end.
Row 8: K3, turn work and cast on 2 sts, turn back again and k to end.
Row 9: K.
Bind (cast) off.

Making up and finishing

Fold the cozy in half widthways and sew up ⅜in. (1cm) with mattress stitch (see page 92) at the top and bottom of each edge, leaving a large gap in the center for the mug handle. For a snug fit, you may want to try the cozy on your mug, because the position of the handle may vary slightly.

Lay the strap over the handle gap with the flat end on the right. Overstitch the flat end in place. Sew the button in position to match the buttonhole.

Egg Cozies

Cheer up your breakfast time with this trio of quirky egg cozies. Use up your scraps of any light worsted (DK) yarn for these, adjusting the needle size if necessary, to make this a great stashbusting project. You don't even have to follow the colors we've used here, just use any suitable colors you have to hand. The cozies are very quick to make and are an ideal Easter gift for friends and family.

YARN AND OTHER MATERIALS

Use any light worsted (DK) yarn with some wool content

For the Bluebird egg cozy:
1 part ball of soft blue (A)
Very small amounts of deep yellow (B) and black (C)

For the Frenchman egg cozy:
1 part ball of red (A)
1 part ball of pale pink (B)
1 part ball of bright blue (C)
Very small amounts of black (D) and dusky pink (E)

For the Blonde Girl egg cozy:
1 part ball of bright turquoise (A)
1 part ball of pale pink (B)
1 part ball of bright pink (C)
Small amount of yellow (D)
Very small amounts of black (E) and red (F)

NEEDLES AND EQUIPMENT

Size US 3 (3.25mm) knitting needles
Yarn sewing needle
Large-eyed embroidery needle
Red coloring pencil

GAUGE (TENSION)

25 sts and 28 rows in stockinette (stocking) stitch to a 4-in (10-cm) square on US 3 (3.25mm) needles.

MEASUREMENTS

All the egg cozies are approx. 2¾in (7cm) tall.

ABBREVIATIONS

approx.	approximately
beg	begin(ning)
k	knit
k2tog	knit two stitches together
p2tog	purl two stitches together
psso	pass slipped stitch over, pass a slipped stitch over another stitch
rem	remain(ing)
sl1	slip one stitch from the left-hand needle to the right-hand needle without knitting it
ssk	slip one stitch, slip one stitch, knit slipped stitches together
st(s)	stitch(es)
st st	stockinette (stocking) stitch
[ ]	work instructions within square brackets as directed

Bluebird

MAIN COZY

(make 1)
Cast on 42 sts in A.
Row 1: K.
Work 20 rows in st st beg with a k row.
Row 22: K2, [sl1, k2tog, psso, k4] 5 times, sl1, k2tog, psso, k2. (30 sts)
Row 23: P.
Row 24: K1, [sl1, k2tog, psso, k2] 5 times, sl1, k2tog, psso, k1. (18 sts)
Row 25: P2tog to end. (9 sts)
Thread yarn through rem sts, pull up tightly, and secure.

WINGS

(make 2)
Cast on 6 sts in A.
Row 1: K.
Row 2: K1, p to last st, k1.
Rep last 2 rows twice more.
Row 7: K1, k2tog, ssk, k1. (4 sts)
Row 8: K1, p2, k1.
Row 9: K2tog, ssk. (2 sts)
Row 10: K2tog.
Break yarn and pull rem st through.

BEAK

(make 1)
Cast on 7 sts in B.
Bind (cast) off.

Making up and finishing

Join the back seam of the cozy using mattress stitch (see page 92). Oversew (see page 91) the wings in position. Fold the beak in half widthwise and oversew it in place.

Work two French knots (see page 93) in C for the eyes.

Frenchman

(make 1)
Cast on 42 sts in A.
Row 1: K.
Work 4 rows in st st beg with a k row.
Break A and join in B.
Work 12 rows in st st beg with a k row.
Break B and join in C.
Work 4 rows in st st beg with a k row.
Row 22: K2, [sl1, k2tog, psso, k4] 5 times, sl1, k2tog, psso, k2. (30 sts)
Row 23: P.
Row 24: K1, [sl1, k2tog, psso, k2] 5 times, sl1, k2tog, psso, k1. (18 sts)
Row 25: P2tog to end. (9 sts)
Row 26: [Sl1, k2tog, psso] 3 times. (3 sts)
Work 3 rows in st st beg with a p row.
Bind (cast) off.

Making up and finishing

Join the back seam of the cozy using mattress stitch (see page 92) and matching yarns.

Work two French knots (see page 93) in D for the eyes. Separate a strand of D and work two straight stitches (see page 93) for the eyebrows. Use another single strand of D to work the moustache in chain stitch (see page 93). Using E, work two small straight stitches, one over the other, for the mouth.

Use the red coloring pencil to color the cheeks.

Blonde Girl

(make 1)
Cast on 42 sts in A.
Row 1: K.
Work 4 rows in st st beg with a k row.
Break A and join in B.
Work 10 rows in st st beg with a k row.
Break B and join in C.
K 2 rows.
Work 4 rows in st st beg with a k row.
Row 22: K2, [sl1, k2tog, psso, k4] 5 times, sl1, k2tog, psso, k2. (30 sts)
Row 23: P.
Row 24: K1, [sl1, k2tog, psso, k2] 5 times, sl1, k2tog, psso, k1. (18 sts)
Row 25: P2tog to end. (9 sts)
Trim yarn, thread through rem sts, and secure.

Making up and finishing

Join the back seam of the cozy using mattress stitch (see page 92) and matching yarns.

Work two French knots (see page 93) in E for the eyes. Separate a strand of E and work three straight stitches (see page 93) above each eye for the eyelashes. Using a separated strand of F, work two straight stitches in a flat V-shape for the mouth.

For the hair, cut six 10-in (25-cm) lengths of D and divide the lengths into two groups each consisting of three lengths. Secure the center of each group to the side of the cozy, just under the "hat." Braid (plait) the yarn lengths and secure the ends.

Use the red coloring pencil to color the cheeks.

YARN AND OTHER MATERIALS

For the white and lilac coaster:
Sublime Baby Cashmere Merino Silk DK
(75% merino wool, 20% silk, 5% cashmere;
127yd/116m per 1¾oz/50g ball) light
worsted (DK) yarn
  1 ball of shade 003 Vanilla (A) (off-white)
  Small amount of shade 357 Tiffany (B)
  (lilac)

For the blue and pink coaster:
Sublime Baby Cashmere Merino Silk DK
(75% merino wool, 20% silk, 5% cashmere;
127yd/116m per 1¾oz/50g ball) light
worsted (DK) yarn
  1 ball of shade 491 Twinkle (A) (pale blue)
  Small amount of shade 001 Piglet (B)
  (pale pink)

For the yellow and green coaster:
Schachenmayr Merino Extrafine 120 (100%
wool; 131yd/120m per 1¾oz/50g ball) light
worsted (DK) yarn
  1 ball of shade 120 Sonne (A) (yellow)
  Small amount of shade 173 Apfel (B)
  (green)

NEEDLES AND EQUIPMENT

Size US 2/3 (3mm) knitting needles

Yarn sewing needle

GAUGE (TENSION)

21 sts and 38 rows in garter stitch to a 4-in
(10-cm) square on US 2/3 (3mm) needles
using yarn double.

MEASUREMENTS

Each finished coaster measures approx.
5¼in (13cm) in diameter.

ABBREVIATIONS

approx.	approximately
beg	begin(ning)
k	knit
k2tog	knit two stitches together
kwise	knitwise
LH	left-hand
p	purl
sl1	slip one stitch from the left-hand needle to the right-hand needle without knitting it
st(s)	stitch(es)
st st	stockinette (stocking) stitch
WS	wrong side(s)
yo	yarnover
[ ]	work instructions within square brackets as directed

Coasters

Everyone needs at least one set of coasters to protect
those favorite pieces of furniture—and what better way
to acquire a set than to knit your own? These coasters
are a brilliant way of using up odds and ends of light
worsted (DK) yarn and a great starter project if you want
to try your hand at knitting circles.

Coaster

Cast on 10 sts in A, using yarn double.
Row 1: K.
Row 2: K9, turn. (1 st left on LH needle)
Row 3: Sl1, k to end.
Row 4: K8, turn. (2 sts left on LH needle)
Row 5: Sl1, k to end.
Row 6: K7, turn. (3 sts left on LH needle)
Row 7: Sl1, k to end.
Row 8: K6, turn. (4 sts left on LH needle)
Row 9: Sl1, k to end.
Row 10: K5, turn. (5 sts left on LH needle)
Row 11: Sl1, k to end.
Row 12: K.
Rep last 12 rows 6 times more.
Bind (cast) off.
Using B double, pick up and k 44 sts along outer edge of coaster.
Work 3 rows in st st beg with a p row.
Next row: K2, [yo, k2tog, k1] to end.
Work 2 rows in st st beg with a p row.
Bind (cast) off kwise (on WS of work).

Making up and finishing

Join the cast-on and bound-(cast-)off edges of the main coaster using flat stitch (see page 91) and join the two short edges of the trim using mattress stitch (see page 92), so the coaster forms a circle.

Turn down the long edge of the trim and oversew (see page 91) in place on the underside so that the holes in the trim form a picot edging.

Soak the coaster thoroughly in lukewarm water, squeeze out the excess, shape the coaster, and dry flat.

YARN AND OTHER MATERIALS

Sublime Baby Cashmere Merino Silk DK
(75% merino wool, 20% silk, 5%
cashmere; 127yd/116m per 1¾oz/50g
ball) light worsted (DK) yarn
  Small amount each of shades:
  527 Diddy Dino (A) (pale green)
  458 Little Liberty (B) (mauve)
  001 Piglet (C) (pale pink)

1 x ½-in (12-mm) green button
1 x ½-in (12-mm) yellow button

NEEDLES AND EQUIPMENT

Size US 2/3 (3mm) knitting needles

Yarn sewing needle

Large-eyed embroidery needle

GAUGE (TENSION)

28 sts and 30 rows in seed (moss) stitch
to a 4-in (10-cm) square on US 2/3
(3mm) needles.

MEASUREMENTS

The napkin rings measure approx. 1¾in
(4.5cm) in diameter.

ABBREVIATIONS

approx.	approximately
beg	begin(ning)
inc	increase
k	knit
k2tog	knit two stitches together
LH	left-hand
p	purl
rem	remain(ing)
rep	repeat
RH	right-hand
ssk	slip one stitch, slip one stitch, knit slipped stitches together
st(s)	stitch(es)
st st	stockinette (stocking) stitch
[ ]	work instructions within square brackets as directed
*	work instructions after/ between asterisk(s) as directed

Napkin Rings

Jazz up your dining table and impress your friends with these funky floral napkin rings. The main napkin ring is knitted in a textured seed (moss) stitch and the flowers are much easier to work than they look. This project is an ideal way of using up your stash, and they are so quick to make you'll be able to knit enough to adorn your table in just a few evenings.

Napkin ring

MAIN PIECE
(make one)
Cast on 11 sts in A or B.
Row 1: K1, [p1, k1] to end.
Rep last row 43 times more.
Bind (cast) off.

FLOWER
(make 1)
Cast on 10 sts in B or C.
Row 1: Inc1 twice.
Turn and work on 4 sts just knitted only.
Work 11 rows in st st beg with a p row.
Next row: K2tog, ssk, lift RH st over LH st. (*1 st*)
*Next row: K1 into next cast-on st, inc1.
Turn and work on 4 sts just worked only.
Work 11 rows in st st beg with a p row.
Next row: K2tog, ssk, lift RH st over LH st.** (*1 st*)
Rep from * to ** 3 more times.
K into first cast-on st to complete final petal. (*2 sts*)
Bind (cast) off 1 st, break yarn, and pull through rem st.

Making up and finishing

Join the back seam of the main piece using mattress stitch (see page 92) and matching yarn.

Stitch the flower in B on the ring in A and the flower in C on the ring in B.

Using the large-eyed embroidery needle, stitch the green button on the C flower using A and the yellow button on the B flower using C.

Potholder

Knitted quite tightly in a heavy wool yarn, this potholder adds a touch of retro charm to your kitchen, and offers excellent protection from those hot pot handles. If you want to use up a different super-bulky (super-chunky) yarn, just make sure the gauge (tension) is tight enough to give a firm fabric. This is an excellent project if you're the sort of person who wants to make something practical as well as decorative.

YARN AND OTHER MATERIALS

Rowan Big Wool (100% wool; 87yd/80m per 3½oz/100g ball) super-bulky (super-chunky) yarn
  1 ball of shade 021 Ice Blue

NEEDLES AND EQUIPMENT

Size US 8 (5mm) knitting needles

Yarn sewing needle

GAUGE (TENSION)

14 sts and 22 rows in main pattern to a 4-in (10-cm) square on US 8 (5mm) needles.

MEASUREMENTS

The potholder measures 8¾in (22cm) square, excluding loop.

ABBREVIATIONS

k	knit
p	purl
rep	repeat
st(s)	stitch(es)
[ ]	work instructions within square brackets as directed

Potholder

MAIN PIECE
(make 1)
Cast on 33 sts.
K 4 rows.
Row 5: K6, [p1, k1, p1, k3] to last 3 sts, k3.
Row 6: K3, p4, k1, [p5, k1] to last 7 sts, p4, k3.
Rep last 2 rows 19 times more.
Row 45: K6, [p1, k1, p1, k3] to last 3 sts, k3.
K 3 rows.
Bind (cast) off.

LOOP
(make 1)
Cast on 22 sts.
Bind (cast) off.

Making up and finishing

Use the two yarn tails on the loop to sew it to one corner of the main piece. Weave in any other yarn ends.

CHAPTER 2

For Baby

Mouse Mittens

Is it a mitten? Is it a glove puppet? It's a little bit of both, of course. These mousey mitts make it as easy as pie to persuade little ones to put on their gloves when the mercury dips, so you won't hear complaints about freezing little fingers. I've chosen to knit these mice in off-white—but I think little mice in gray, or in pastel shades of pink or blue, would be just as cute. So take your pick.

YARN AND OTHER MATERIALS

Sublime Baby Cashmere Merino Silk DK (75% merino wool, 20% silk, 5% cashmere; 127yd/116m per 1¾oz/50g ball) light worsted (DK) yarn

   1 ball of shade 048 Cheeky (A) (pink)
   1 ball of shade 344 Little Linen (B) (off-white)

Very small amount of any light worsted (DK) yarn in black

NEEDLES AND EQUIPMENT

US 3 (3.25mm) knitting needles

US 6 (4mm) knitting needles

Yarn sewing needle

Large-eyed embroidery needle

GAUGE (TENSION)

22 sts and 28 rows in stockinette (stocking) stitch to a 4-in (10-cm) square on US 6 (4mm) needles.

MEASUREMENTS

To fit an average 12–18 month (2–3 year) old toddler.
The palm of the mitten is 4(4½)in/ 10(11.5)cm from the top of the rib section to the end of the mitten and is 4¾(5¼)in/12(13.5)cm around the hand.

ABBREVIATIONS

beg	begin(ning)
k	knit
k2tog	knit two stitches together
LH	left-hand
inc	increase
inc pwise	increase on a purl row
m1	make one stitch
p	purl
p2tog	purl two stitches together
rep	repeat
RH	right-hand
RS	right side(s)
ssk	slip one stitch, slip one stitch, knit slipped stitches together
st(s)	stitch(es)
st st	stockinette (stocking) stitch
WS	wrong side(s)
[ ]	work instructions within square brackets as directed
*	work instructions after/ between asterisk(s) as directed

Mittens

RIGHT MITTEN

Using US 3 (3.25mm) needles cast on 28(30) sts in A.

Size 12–18 months only

Row 1: [K2, p2] to end.

Row 2: [K2, p2] to end.

Rep rows 1–2 four times more.

Size 2–3 years only

Row 1: [K2, p2] to last 2 sts, k2.

Row 2: [P2, k2] to last 2 sts, p2.

Rep rows 1–2 four times more.

Both sizes

Break A, join in B and switch to US 6 (4mm) needles.

Beg with a k row, work 2 rows in st st.*

Row 13: K15(16), m1, k1, m1, k to end. *(30(32) sts)*

Row 14 and every WS row unless otherwise stated: P.

Row 15: K15(16), m1, k3, m1, k to end. *(32(34) sts)*

Row 17: K15(16), m1, k5, m1, k to end. *(34(36) sts)*

Row 19: K15(16), m1, k7, m1, k to end. *(36(38) sts)*

Row 21: K24(25), turn.

Row 22: P9, turn.

Beg with a k row, work 6 rows in st st on 9 sts just worked.

Next row: [Ssk] twice, k1, [k2tog] twice. *(5 sts)*

Break yarn and thread it through rem sts.

**With RS of work facing, put the last st on the RH needle (the st nearest the center) onto the LH needle. Rejoin yarn to sts on LH needle.

Next row: [Inc] twice, k to end.

Now work across all 29(31) sts.

Beg with a p row, work 13(17) rows in st st.

Next row: K2, ssk, k7(8), k2tog, k3, ssk, k7(8), k2tog, k2. *(25(27) sts)*

Next and every WS row unless otherwise stated: P.

Next RS row: K2, ssk, k5(6), k2tog, k3, ssk, k5(6), k2tog, k2. *(21(23) sts)*

Next RS row: [K2tog] 5(6) times, k3(1), [k2tog] 4(5) times. *(12 sts)*

Next row: [P2tog] 6 times. *(6 sts)*

Break yarn and thread through rem sts.

LEFT MITTEN

Work as for right mitten to *.

Row 13: K12(13), m1, k1, m1, k to end. *(30(32) sts)*

Row 14 and every WS row unless otherwise stated: P.

Row 15: K12(13), m1, k3, m1, k to end. *(32(34) sts)*

Row 17: K12(13), m1, k5, m1, k to end. *(34(36) sts)*

Row 19: K12(13), m1, k7, m1, k to end. *(36(38) sts)*

Row 21: K21(22), turn.

Row 22: P9, turn.

Beg with a k row, 6 rows in st st on 9 sts just worked.

Next row: [Ssk] twice, k1, [k2tog] twice. *(5 sts)*

Break yarn and thread it through rem sts.

Work as for right mitten from ** to end.

EARS

(make 4, 2 for each mitten)

Using US 3 (3.25mm) needles, cast on 4 sts in B.

Row 1: [Inc, k1] twice. *(6 sts)*

Beg with a p row, work 3 rows in st st.

Row 5: Ssk, k2, k2tog. *(4 sts)*

Row 6: [P2tog] twice. *(2 sts)*

Row 7: [Inc] twice. *(4 sts)*

Row 8: [Inc pwise, p1] twice. *(6 sts)*

Beg with a k row, work 3 rows in st st.

Row 12: P2tog, p2, p2tog. *(4 sts)*

Bind (cast) off.

Making up and finishing

Join thumb and mitten seams using mattress stitch (see page 92).

Fold ears so that the right sides are on the inside and oversew (see page 91) round curved edges, leaving the lower edges open. Turn the right way out and slip stitch the lower edge together, then pinch them in half and secure. Oversew in position using the photograph as a guide.

Using A, work a small coil of chain stitch (see page 93) for the nose. Using the black yarn, work two large French knots (see page 93) for the eyes.

Weave in all loose ends.

Cow Print Bib

There's no point in facing the world in some boring old bib when you can sport a unique animal print look instead. That's the thinking behind this cow-print creation, which also happens to be a great way to dip your toe into the world of intarsia color knitting. Of course, you could also knit the bib in a single color if you like, or use it as a template to create a range of other animal looks to suit the colors you have in your stash.

YARN AND MATERIALS

Sublime Extra Fine Merino DK (100% wool; 127yd/116m per 1¾oz/50g ball) light worsted (DK) yarn
   1 ball each of shades:
   003 Alabaster (A) (off-white)
   013 Jet Black (B)

1 x ½-in (11-mm) snap fastener

Standard white sewing thread

NEEDLES AND EQUIPMENT

US 6 (4mm) knitting needles

US G/6 or H/8 (4.5mm) crochet hook (or one of a similar size)

Yarn sewing needle

Standard sewing needle

GAUGE (TENSION)

22 sts and 28 rows in stockinette (stocking) stitch to a 4-in (10-cm) square on US 6 (4mm) needles.

MEASUREMENTS

To fit a baby up to 12 months old.
Bib measures 7½in (19cm) wide at the top edge and 6½in (16.5cm) deep at the front.

ABBREVIATIONS

beg	begin(ning)
inc	increase
k	knit
k2tog	knit two stitches together
m1	make one stitch
p	purl
p2tog	purl two stitches together
rem	remain(ing)
RS	right side(s)
ssk	slip one stitch, slip one stitch, knit slipped stitches together
st(s)	stitch(es)
st st	stockinette (stocking) stitch
WS	wrong side(s)

Bib

Start at bottom edge

Cast on 28 sts in A.

Row 1: Inc, k to last 2 sts, inc, k1. (*30 sts*)

Row 2: P.

Row 3: K2, m1, k to last 2 sts, m1, k2. (*32 sts*)

Row 4: P.

Row 5: K2, m1, k to last 2 sts, m1, k2. (*34 sts*)

Row 6: Join in B and work row 6 from first row of chart, opposite.

This row sets position of chart.

Follow chart to row 48, increasing 1 st on each RS row up to and including row 15, and using a separate length of B for each black patch. (*44 sts*)

Break all B and cont in A.

Beg with a k row, work 4 rows in st st.

Next row: K15, ssk, turn. (*16 sts*)

Work on 16 sts just worked only, leaving rem sts on needle.

Next row: P2tog, p to end. (*15 sts*)

Next row: K13, ssk. (*14 sts*)

Next row: P2tog, p to end. (*13 sts*)

Next row: K11, ssk. (*12 sts*)

Next and every WS row: Purl.

Next RS row: K10, ssk. (*11 sts*)

Next RS row: K9, ssk. (*10 sts*)

Next RS row: K8, ssk. (*9 sts*)

Next RS row: K7, ssk. (*8 sts*)

Next row: P.

Beg with a k row, work 10 rows in st st.

Next row: K2, k2tog, k2, m1, k2.

Beg with a p row, work 3 rows in st st.

Rep last 4 rows once more.

Beg with a k row, work 6 rows in st st.

Next row: K1, k2tog, k2, ssk, k1. (*6 sts*)

Next row: P2tog, p2, p2tog. (*4 sts*)

Bind (cast) off.

Rejoin yarn to RS of work.

Bind (cast) off 11 sts, k to end. (*16 sts*)

Next row: P to last 2 sts, p2tog. (*15 sts*)

Next row: K2tog, k to end. (*14 sts*)

Next row: P to last 2 sts, p2tog. (*13 sts*)

Next row: K2tog, k to end. (*12 sts*)

Next row: P.

Rep last 2 rows four times more. (*8 sts*)

Beg with a k row, work 10 rows in st st.

Next row: K2, m1, k2, ssk, k2.

Beg with a p row, work 3 rows in st st.

Rep last 4 rows once more.

Beg with a k row, work 6 rows in st st.
Next row: K1, k2tog, k2, ssk, k1. (*6 sts*)
Next row: P2tog, p2, p2tog. (*4 sts*)
Bind (cast) off.

Making up and finishing

Using crochet hook and B double, work an even crochet edging (see page 94) around entire bib.

Sew one part of the snap fastener on the right side of one neck strap. Sew the other part of the snap fastener to the wrong side of the second neck strap so that the strap will fasten around the baby's neck.

Weave in all loose ends.

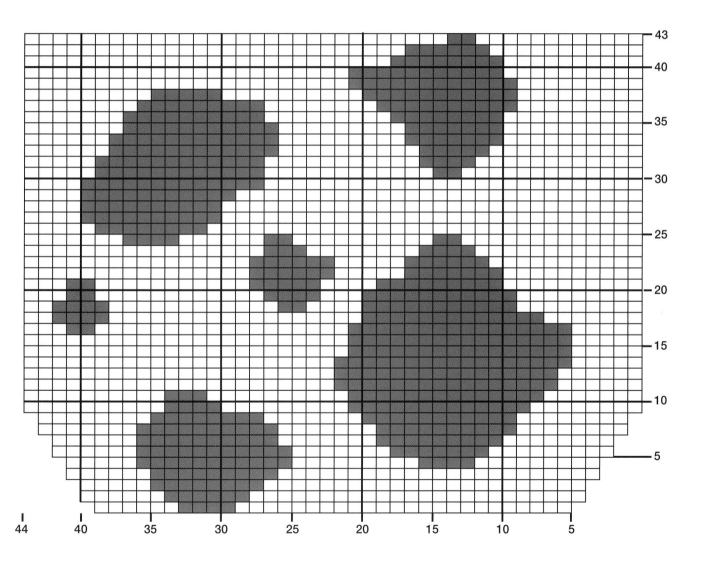

☐ Alabaster (A)
▨ Black (B)

Tiger Hat

Big cats don't come much more docile than this. This tiger hat is knitted in Debbie Bliss Baby Cashmerino, but any baby yarn of a similar weight could work if the gauge (tension) matches.

YARN AND OTHER MATERIALS

Debbie Bliss Baby Cashmerino (55% wool, 33% acrylic, 12% cashmere; 137yd/125m per 1¾oz/50g ball) sport weight (light DK) yarn
  1 ball of shade 067 Sienna (A) (orange)
  1 part ball of shade 300 Black (B)

Small amount of standard sewing thread

NEEDLES AND EQUIPMENT

US 3 (3.25mm) knitting needles

Yarn sewing needle

GAUGE (TENSION)

25 sts and 34 rows in stockinette (stocking) stitch to a 4-in (10-cm) square on US 3 (3.25mm) needles. Note that if you are considering substituting the yarn, this yarn is like a thin light worsted (DK) and knits up well on these size needles.

MEASUREMENTS

To fit an average 3–6 month (9–12 month) old baby.
Hat circumference is 13(15)in/ 33(38)cm.

ABBREVIATIONS

beg	begin(ning)
k	knit
k2tog	knit two stitches together
p	purl
p2tog	purl two stitches together
ssk	slip one stitch, slip one stitch, knit slipped stitches together
st(s)	stitch(es)
st st	stockinette (stocking) stitch
WS	wrong side
[ ]	work instructions within square brackets as directed

Hat

MAIN PIECE
Using US 3 (3.25mm) needles, cast on 84(96) sts in A.
Beg with a k row, work 10(14) rows in st st.
Beg with a k row, work 2 rows in st st in B.
Beg with a k row, work 6 rows in st st in A.
Rep last 8 rows twice more.
Beg with a k row, work 2 rows in st st in B.
Beg with a k row, work 4 rows in st st in A.
Now, working 2 rows st st in A, 2 rows st st in B, then breaking B and working rest of hat in A, AT THE SAME TIME shape crown as folls:
Size 9–12 months only
Next row: [K6, k2tog] to end. *(84 sts)*
Next row: P.
Both sizes
Next row: [K5, k2tog] to end. *(72 sts)*
Next and every foll WS row unless otherwise stated: P.
Next RS row: [K4, k2tog] to end. *(60 sts)*
Next RS row: [K3, k2tog] to end. *(48 sts)*
Next RS row: [K2, k2tog] to end. *(36 sts)*
Next RS row: [K1, k2tog] to end. *(24 sts)*
Next RS row: [K2tog] to end. *(12 sts)*
Next row: [P2tog] to end. *(6 sts)*
Break yarn and thread through rem sts.

EARS
(make 4)
Using US 3 (3.25mm) needles, cast on 8 sts in A.
Beg with a k row, work 6 rows in st st.
Row 7: K1, ssk, k2, k2tog, k1. *(6 sts)*
Row 8: P2tog, p2, p2tog. *(4 sts)*
Bind (cast) off.

Making up and finishing

Sew the back seam of the hat using mattress stitch (see page 92).

Place two ear pieces right sides together and oversew (see page 91) round the curved edges. Turn the right way out and slip stitch the cast-on edges together. Make the other ear in the same way. Oversew the ears in position using the photograph as a guide.

Weave in all loose ends.

YARN AND OTHER MATERIALS

Debbie Bliss Baby Cashmerino (55% wool, 33% acrylic, 12% cashmere; 137yd/125m per 1¾oz/50g ball) sport weight (light DK) yarn
  1 ball of shade 094 Rose Pink (A)
  1 part ball of shade 101 Ecru (B)

Small amount of light worsted (DK) yarn in black

NEEDLES AND EQUIPMENT

US 7 (4.5mm) knitting needles

Yarn sewing needle

Large-eyed embroidery needle

GAUGE (TENSION)

18 sts and 26 rows in stockinette (stocking) stitch to a 4-in (10-cm) square on US 7 (4.5mm) needles with yarn used double.

MEASUREMENTS

To fit an average 0–6 month (6–12 month) old baby. Length of the sole is 3¼(3¾)in/(8.25(9.5)cm).

ABBREVIATIONS

beg	begin(ning)
k	knit
k2tog	knit two stitches together
LH	left-hand
p	purl
psso	pass slipped stitch(es) over
rem	remain(ing)
RS	right side(s)
sl1	slip one stitch from the left-hand needle to the right-hand needle without knitting it
ssk	slip one stitch, slip one stitch, knit slipped stitches together
st(s)	stitch(es)
st st	stockinette (stocking) stitch
[ ]	work instructions within square brackets as directed

Rabbit Bootees

These soft pastel bunny bootees are guaranteed to keep little feet looking good as well as feeling cozy. Bootees are much easier to knit than socks, and I reckon they're a great project to try if you've mastered simpler items like hats and feel like moving on. And if you use a different yarn and they turn out a bit larger, then you won't have to wait long for baby to grow into them!

Bootees

MAIN PART
(make 2)
Cast on 28(30) sts in A, using yarn double.
Row 1: K0(2), [p2, k2] to end.
Row 2: [P2, k2] to last 0(2) sts, p0(2).
Rep rows 1–2 five times more.
Row 13: K19(20), turn.
Row 14: P10, turn. Cont working on these center 10 sts, leaving the other sts on the right-and left-hand needles.
Beg with a k row, work 12(14) rows in st st.
Leave these 10 sts on holder and break yarn.
With RS facing, rejoin yarn to right-hand edge at base of rectangle just worked, at inner edge of 9 (10) sts on right-hand needle.
Using the right-hand needle, pick up and k 7(8) sts up first side, k across 10 sts on holder, pick up and k 7(8) sts down second side, k rem 9(10) sts. *(42(46) sts)*
Beg with a p row, work 3 rows in st st.
Next row: K3, k2tog, k to last 5 sts, ssk, k3. *(40(44) sts)*
Next row: K.
Break A and join in B, using it double.
Rep last 2 rows once more. *(38(42) sts)*
Next row: K3, k2tog, k10(12), ssk, k4, k2tog, k10(12), ssk, k3. *(34(38) sts)*
Next row: K.
Next row: K3, k2tog, k8(10), ssk, k4, k2tog, k8(10), ssk, k3. *(30(34) sts)*
Next row: K.
Next row: K3, k2tog, k6(8), ssk, k4, k2tog, k6(8), ssk, k3. *(26(30) sts)*
Next row: K.
Bind (cast) off.

EARS
(make 4, 2 for each bootee)
Cast on 3 sts in A, using yarn double.
K 16 rows.
Row 17: Sl1, k2tog, psso. *(1 st)*
Fasten off.

Making up and finishing

Sew the back and sole seam using flat stitch (see page 91).

Oversew the ears in position using the photograph as
a guide.

Using the black yarn, work two small circles of chain
stitches (see page 93) or French knots (see page 93) for
the eyes. Work the nose and mouth in straight stitch (see
page 93) using the photograph as a guide.

Weave in all loose ends.

Hanging Birds

This delicate trio are knitted in baby-friendly shades and, because each bird uses such a small amount, they're a great way of using up any small leftovers. I loved knitting them so much and they come together so quickly, I was tempted to knit a flock. I hope you love them too, and that you'll think up lots of ways of using them to decorate a baby's room.

YARN AND OTHER MATERIALS

Cascade Cherub DK (55% nylon, 45% acrylic; 180yd/165m per 1¾oz/50g ball) light worsted (DK) yarn
    1 part ball each of shades:
    13 Jade (A) (blue-green)
    53 Mauve Orchid (B) (mauve)
    28 Boy Blue (C) (pale blue)
    17 Grey (D) for the cord and tassel

Very small amounts of black and yellow light worsted (DK) yarns

Few handfuls of 100% polyester toy filling

NEEDLES AND EQUIPMENT

US 3 (3.25mm) knitting needles

US D/3 (3.25mm) crochet hook (or one of a similar size)

Yarn sewing needle

Large-eyed embroidery needle

GAUGE (TENSION)

25 sts and 34 rows in stockinette (stocking) stitch to a 4-in (10-cm) square on US 3 (3.25mm) needles.

MEASUREMENTS

Each bird measures approx. 3½in (9cm) across.

ABBREVIATIONS

approx.	approximately
beg	begin(ning)
inc	increase
k	knit
k2tog	knit two stitches together
m1	make one stitch
p	purl
p2tog	purl two stitches together
pwise	purlwise
rep	repeat
RS	right side(s)
ssk	slip one stitch, slip one stitch, knit slipped stitches together
st(s)	stitch(es)
st st	stockinette (stocking) stitch
*****	work instructions after/ between asterisk(s) as directed

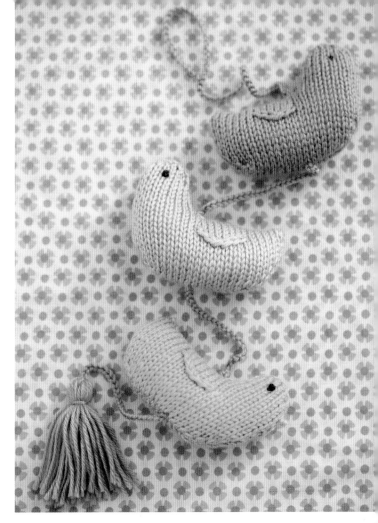

Bird

(make 3, one in each of A, B, and C)

FIRST SIDE

Cast on 15 sts.
Row 1: Inc, k to last 2 sts, inc, k1. *(17 sts)*
Row 2: P.
Row 3: K1, m1, k to last st, m1, k1. *(19 sts)*
Row 4: P.
Rep rows 3–4 three times more.* *(25 sts)*
Beg with a k row, work 6 rows in st st.
Row 17: Bind (cast) off 14 sts, k to end. *(11 sts)*
Beg with a p row, work 5 rows in st st.
**Row 23: K1, k2tog, k to last 3 sts, ssk, k1. *(9 sts)*
Row 24: P2tog, p5, p2tog. *(7 sts)*
Row 25: K1, k2tog, k1, ssk, k1. *(5 sts)*
Bind (cast) off pwise.

SECOND SIDE

Work as for first side to *.
Beg with a k row, work 5 rows in st st.
Row 16: Bind (cast) off 14 sts pwise, p to end. *(11 sts)*
Beg with a k row, work 6 rows in st st.
Work as for first side from ** to end.

Cords

Using the crochet hook and D, make four lengths of crochet chain (see page 94), one 8-in (20-cm) long chain for the top and three 3-in (8-cm) long chains. Leave tails of yarn at the start and end of each chain for sewing.

Tassel

Using D, wrap yarn around four fingers approximately 20 times. Ease the yarn off fingers and cut the loops once to make a bundle of yarn lengths. Tie the yarn tail from one of the smaller chain lengths (see above) around the center of the lengths, so the chain butts right up to the lengths. Hold the chain so that the lengths hang downward. Tie a short length of gray yarn round the lengths, about ½in (1cm) down from the top of the tassel, tying it as tightly as possible. Trim the yarn loops to complete the tassel.

Making up and finishing

Place the two pieces for each bird RS together. Oversew (see page 91) around the outer edge, leaving the lower edge open for turning and stuffing. Turn the piece RS out. Stuff fairly lightly and close the lower edge using mattress stitch (see page 92).

Using the yarn double, embroider the wings in chain stitch (see page 93) using the photograph as a guide. Using black yarn, work French knots (see page 93) for the eyes. Using yellow yarn, work French knots for the beaks.

Join the birds together with the lengths of crochet chain, sewing the tails of yarn at the ends of the chains to the tops and bottoms of the birds. Make sure the long length is attached to the top bird and the tassel is at the bottom. Form the free end of the top length into a loop for hanging.

Weave in all loose ends.

YARN AND OTHER MATERIALS

Debbie Bliss Cashmerino Aran (55% wool, 33% acrylic, 12% cashmere; 98yd/90m per 1¾oz/50g ball) worsted (Aran) yarn
  1 ball of shade 073 Coral (A)

Drops Air (70% alpaca, 23% nylon, 7% wool; 142yd/130m) worsted (Aran) yarn
  1 part ball of shade 01 Off White (B)

Small amount of light beige worsted (Aran) yarn (C)

Very small amount of black light worsted (DK) yarn

Few handfuls of 100% polyester toy filling

NEEDLES AND EQUIPMENT

Size US 8 (5mm) knitting needles

Size US 7 (4.5mm) knitting needles

Size US 6 (4mm) knitting needles

Yarn sewing needle

Large-eyed embroidery needle

GAUGE (TENSION)

18 sts and 24 rows in stockinette (stocking) stitch to a 4-in (10-cm) square on US 8 (5mm) needles for A.
18 sts and 24 rows in stockinette (stocking) stitch to a 4-in (10-cm) square on US 7 (4.5mm) needles for B.

MEASUREMENTS

The blanket is approx. 10 x 10in (25 x 25cm).
It is safe for children from birth onward, so long as all parts are very firmly secured.

ABBREVIATIONS

approx.	approximately
beg	begin(ning)
inc	increase
k	knit
k2tog	knit two stitches together
m1	make one stitch
p	purl
p2sso	pass two slipped stitches over
p2tog	purl wo stitches together
rem	remain(ing)
rep	repeat
sl2	slip two stitches from the left-hand needle to the right-hand needle without knitting them
ssk	slip one stitch, slip one stitch, knit slipped stitches together
st(s)	stitch(es)
st st	stockinette (stocking) stitch
[ ]	work instructions within square brackets as directed

Lamb Snuggle Blanket

Comfort blankets are a great way to help babies settle, so here I'd like to introduce a blanket with all the traditional attributes, plus a bit more personality. I've knitted the main blanket in one of my favorite but oh-so-easy to work textures. And I've used a soft luxury yarn with a touch of cashmere that comes in a range of adorable shades, but any soft yarn of the same weight should work, as exact size is less important than the snuggle-factor for this make.

Blanket

Using US 8 (5mm) needles, cast on 40 sts in A.
K 4 rows.
Row 5: K4, [p2, k1] to last 3 sts, k3.
Row 6: K3, [p1, k2] to last 4 sts, p1, k3.
Row 7: K.
Row 8: K3, p to last 3 sts, k3.
Rep rows 5–8 fourteen times more.
Rep rows 5–6 once more.
K 4 rows.
Bind (cast) off.

Lamb

HEAD
Using US 7 (4.5mm) needles, cast on 7 sts in B.
Row 1: [Inc] to end. *(14 sts)*
Row 2: K.
Row 3: [K2, m1] to last 2 sts, k2. *(20 sts)*
Row 4: K.
Rep rows 3–4 once more. *(29 sts)*
K 5 rows.
Break yarn, join in C, and change to US 6 (4mm) needles.
Beg with a k row, work 6 rows in st st.
Row 18: K2, ssk, k4, sl2, k1, p2sso, k7, sl2, k1, p2sso, k4, k2tog, k2. *(23 sts)*
Row 19: P.
Row 20: K2, [ssk] twice, sl2, k1, p2sso, k5, sl2, k1, p2sso, [k2tog] twice, k2. *(15 sts)*
Row 21: P2tog, p to last 2 sts, p2tog. *(13 sts)*
Row 22: K2, [ssk] twice, k1, [k2tog] twice, k2. *(9 sts)*
Break yarn, thread through rem sts, and secure.

EARS
(make 2)
Using US 6 (4mm) needles, cast on 4 sts in B.
K 4 rows.
Row 5: Ssk, k2tog. *(2 sts)*
Row 6: K2tog. *(1 st)*
Fasten off.

ARMS
(make 2)
Using US 7 (4.5mm) needles, cast on 7 sts in B.
Beg with a k row, work 14 rows in st st.
Break yarn, join in C, and change to US 6 (4mm) needles.
Beg with a k row, work 3 rows in st st.
Row 18: P2tog, p3, p2tog. *(5 sts)*
Break yarn, thread through rem sts, and secure.

Making up and finishing

Fold the head piece in half so the right side is on the outside and the row ends meet. Join this seam using flat stitch (see page 91), leaving the cast-on edge open for stuffing. Stuff head fairly firmly and close gap.

Sew the ears in place.

Using black yarn, work two French knots (see page 93) for the eyes and a "Y" shape in straight stitch (see page 93) for the nose.

Sew the long seam of the arms using mattress stitch (see page 92) and matching yarns, leaving the short edge open. Stuff lightly. Stitch the cast-on edge of the arms in place on the center of the blanket, so they point to opposite corners.

Sew the head in place.

Weave in all loose ends.

Penguin Toy

While teddies are lovely, I wanted to do something a little different, so I created this endearing penguin, complete with wooly scarf to keep out the seasonal chills. Because his eyes are embroidered he's completely safe for babies—but make sure you remove his scarf first and double-check that all the small parts are very securely stitched on.

YARN AND OTHER MATERIALS

Lion Brand Wool Ease (80% acrylic, 20% wool; 196yd/180m per 3oz/80g ball) worsted (Aran) yarn
  1 ball of shade 099 Fisherman (A) (white)
  1 ball of shade 153 Black (B)

Small amount of bright yellow light worsted (DK) yarn (C)

Small amount of light worsted (DK) yarn in color of your choice for scarf (D)

Approx. 1oz (just over 25g) 100% polyester toy filling

NEEDLES AND EQUIPMENT

US 6 (4mm) knitting needles

US 3 (3.25mm) knitting needles

US 5 (3.75mm) needles

Yarn sewing needle

Large-eyed embroidery needle

GAUGE (TENSION)

18 sts and 26 rows in stockinette (stocking) stitch to a 4-in (10-cm) square on US 6 (4mm) needles.

MEASUREMENTS

The penguin toy is 7in (18cm) tall.

ABBREVIATIONS

beg	begin(ning)
inc	increase
k	knit
k2tog	knit two stitches together
m1	make one stitch
p	purl
p2tog	purl two stitches together
rep	repeat
RS	right side(s)
ssk	slip one stitch, slip one stitch, knit slipped stitches together
st(s)	stitch(es)
st st	stockinette (stocking) stitch
yo	yarnover
[ ]	work instructions within square brackets as directed

Penguin

BODY FRONT

Using US 6 (4mm) needles, cast on 12 sts in A.
Row 1: Inc, k to last 2 sts, inc, k1. *(14 sts)*
Row 2: P.
Row 3: K1, m1, k to last st, m1, k1. *(16 sts)*
Row 4: P.
Rep rows 3–4 once more. *(18 sts)*
Beg with a k row, work 22 rows in st st.
Row 29: K2, ssk, k to last 4 sts, k2tog, k2. *(16 sts)*
Row 30: P.
Rep rows 29–30 once more. *(14 sts)*
Bind (cast) off.

BODY BACK

Using US 6 (4mm) needles, cast on 12 sts in B.
Row 1: Inc, k to last 2 sts, inc, k1. *(14 sts)*
Row 2: P.
Row 3: K1, m1, k to last st, m1, k1. *(16 sts)*
Row 4: P.
Rep rows 3–4 twice more. *(20 sts)*
Beg with a k row, work 20 rows in st st.
Row 29: K2, ssk, k to last 4 sts, k2tog, k2. *(18 sts)*
Row 30: P.
Rep rows 29–30 once more. *(16 sts)*
Bind (cast) off.

HEAD FRONT

Before you begin, wind off a separate 1yd (1m) length of B.
Using US 6 (4mm) needles, cast on 14 sts in A.
Row 1: Inc, k2, inc, k5, inc, k2, inc, k1. *(18 sts)*
Beg with a p row, work 5 rows in st st.
Row 7: K7 in A, k4 in B, k in A (from center of ball) to end.
Row 8: P6 in A, p6 in B (from wound-off length), p in A to end.

Row 9: K6 in A, k6 in B, k in A to end.
Row 10: P6 in A, p6 in B, p in A to end.
Row 11: K5 in A, k8 in B, k in A to end.
Row 12: P2 in B (from main ball), p2 in A, p10 in B, p2 in A, p2 in B (from center of ball).
Break all yarns except for leading B.
Beg with a k row, work 4 rows in st st.
Row 17: K2, [ssk] twice, k6, [k2tog] twice, k2. *(14 sts)*
Row 18: P2tog, p to last 2 sts, p2tog. *(12 sts)*
Bind (cast) off.

HEAD BACK

Using US 6 (4mm) needles, cast on 16 sts in B.
Row 1: Inc, k2, inc, k7, inc, k2, inc, k1. *(20 sts)*
Beg with a p row, work 15 rows in st st.
Row 17: K2, [ssk] 3 times, k4, [k2tog] 3 times, k2. *(14 sts)*
Row 18: P2tog, p to last 2 sts, p2tog. *(12 sts)*
Bind (cast) off.

WINGS

(make 2)
Using US 6 (4mm) needles, cast on 10 sts in B.
Beg with a k row, work 8 rows in st st.
Row 9: K1, ssk, k to last 3 sts, k2tog, k1. *(8 sts)*
Row 10: P.
Rep rows 9–10 once more. *(6 sts)*
Row 13: K1, ssk, k2tog, k1. *(4 sts)*
Row 14: [P2tog] twice. *(2 sts)*
Row 15: K2tog. *(1 st)*
Fasten off.

BEAK

Using US 3 (3.25mm) needles, cast on 10 sts in C.
Beg with a k row, work 2 rows in st st.
Row 3: K2, k2tog, k2, ssk, k2. *(8 sts)*
Row 4: P.
Row 5: K1, k2tog, k2, ssk, k1. *(6 sts)*
Row 6: P2tog, p2, p2tog. *(4 sts)*
Break yarn and thread through rem sts.

FEET

(make 2)
Using US 3 (3.25mm) needles, cast on 6 sts in C.
Beg with a k row, work 6 rows in st st.
Row 7: K2tog, [yo, k2tog] twice. *(5 sts)*
Beg with a p row, work 7 rows in st st.
Bind (cast) off.

Scarf

Using US 5 (3.75mm) needles, cast on 5 sts in D.
K 110 rows.
Bind (cast) off.

Making up and finishing

Weave in all loose ends.

Join the head front to the head back using mattress stitch (see page 92), leaving the lower edges open. Join the front and back body pieces in the same way, leaving the top edges open. Stuff the pieces and join together using mattress stitch, pulling the yarn quite tightly to create the penguin's neck.

Fold the wings in half lengthwise so that the right side is facing outward and slip stitch along the top and the long edge. Oversew (see page 91) in place, just to the front of the side seams.

Fold the beak in half so that the RS is facing outward. Oversew the long seam, stuff lightly, and oversew in place.

Fold the feet in half widthwise so that the "holes" along the middle form the toes. Oversew around the edges, then oversew in place on the underside of the penguin.

Using B, work two small coils of chain stitch (see page 93) for the eyes. Work a coil in A around the outside of each eye.

Tie scarf around neck.

Aardvark Toy

This little knitted African mammal would make a great companion for anyone who finds teddies and bunnies… well, just a little too cute. I've chosen a deep mauve wool-mix yarn for this one, but you could knit him (or her) in any color you want. Aardvarks are a great way of using up oddments in your stash, so why not knit yourself a whole family?

YARN AND OTHER MATERIALS

Sirdar Country Style DK (40% nylon, 30% wool, 30% acrylic; 170yd/155m per 1¾oz/50g ball) light worsted (DK) yarn
  1 ball of shade 615 Purple Sage

Very small amounts of black and white light worsted (DK) yarn

Few handfuls of 100% polyester toy filling

NEEDLES AND EQUIPMENT

US 3 (3.25mm) knitting needles

2 x stitch markers or small safety pins

Yarn sewing needle

Large-eyed embroidery needle

GAUGE (TENSION)

24 sts and 32 rows in stockinette (stocking) stitch to a 4-in (10-cm) square on US 3 (3.25mm) needles.

MEASUREMENTS

The finished toy is 8in (20cm) long (excluding tail).

ABBREVIATIONS

beg	begin(ning)
k	knit
k2tog	knit two stitches together
m1	make one stitch
p	purl
p2tog	purl two stitches together
p3tog	purl three stitches together
pwise	purlwise
rem	remaining
rep	repeat
ssk	slip one stitch, slip one stitch, knit slipped stitches together
st(s)	stitch(es)
st st	stockinette (stocking) stitch
[ ]	work instructions within square brackets as directed
*	work instructions after/ between asterisk(s) as directed

Aardvark

FIRST SIDE
Cast on 6 sts for front leg.
Beg with a k row, work 8 rows in st st.
Row 9: K1, m1, k to last st, m1, k1. *(8 sts)*
Row 10: P.
Rep rows 9–10 once more. *(10 sts)*
Break yarn and leave sts on needle.
On needle with sts, cast on another 6 sts for back leg.
Beg with a k row, work 6 rows in st st.
Row 7: K to last st, m1, k1. *(7 sts)*
Row 8: P.
Rep rows 7–8 once more. *(8 sts)*
Next row: K8 sts from back leg, turn work and cast on 16 sts, turn work back and k9 from front leg, m1, k1. *(35 sts)*
Next row: P.
Next row: K to last 2 sts, m1, k1, m1, k1. *(37 sts)*
Next row: P.*
Rep last 2 rows twice more. *(41 sts)*
Next row: K to last 2 sts, m1, k1, m1, k1. *(43 sts)*
Next row: Cast on 12 sts at beg of row, p to end. *(55 sts)*
Beg with a k row, work 5 rows in st st.

Next row: Bind (cast) off 4 sts pwise, p to end. *(51 sts)*
Next row: K2, k2tog, k to end. *(50 sts)*
Next row: Bind (cast) off 4 sts pwise, p to end. *(46 sts)*
Next row: K.
Next row: Bind (cast) off 4 sts pwise, p to end. *(42 sts)*
Next row: K2, k2tog, k to end. *(41 sts)*
Next row: Bind (cast) off 4 sts pwise, p to end. *(37 sts)*
Next row: K2, k2tog, k to end. *(36 sts)*
Next row: Bind (cast) off 4 sts pwise, p to end. *(32 sts)*
Next row: Bind (cast) off 4 sts, k to end. *(28 sts)*
Next row: Bind (cast) off 4 sts pwise, p to end. *(24 sts)*
Bind (cast) off.

SECOND SIDE

Cast on 6 sts for back leg.
Beg with a k row, work 6 rows in st st.
Row 7: K1, m1, k to end. *(7 sts)*
Row 8: P.
Rep rows 7–8 once more. *(8 sts)*
Break yarn and leave sts on needle.
On needle with sts, cast on another 6 sts for front leg.
Beg with a k row, work 8 rows in st st.
Row 9: K1, m1, k to last st, m1, k1. *(8 sts)*
Row 10: P.
Rep last 2 rows once more. *(10 sts)*
Next row: K1, m1, k rem 9 sts from front leg, turn work and cast on 16 sts, turn work back and k8 from back leg. *(35 sts)*
Next row: P.

Next row: [K1, m1] twice, k to end. *(37 sts)*
Next row: P.
Rep last 2 rows twice more. *(41 sts)*
Next row: [K1, m1] twice, k to end. *(43 sts)*
Next row: P.
Next row: Cast on 12 sts at beg of row, k to end. *(55 sts)*
Beg with a p row, work 5 rows in st st.
Next row: Bind (cast) off 4 sts, k to last 4 sts, ssk, k2. *(50 sts)*
Next row: P.
Next row: Bind (cast) off 4 sts, k to end. *(46 sts)*
Next row: P.
Next row: Bind (cast) off 4 sts, k to last 4 sts, ssk, k2. *(41 sts)*
Next row: P.
Next row: Bind (cast) off 4 sts, k to last 4 sts, ssk, k2. *(36 sts)*
Next row: Bind (cast) off 4 sts pwise, p to end. *(32 sts)*
Next row: Bind (cast) off 4 sts, k to end. *(28 sts)*
Next row: Bind (cast) off 4 sts pwise, p to end. *(24 sts)*
Bind (cast) off.

GUSSET

Work as for first side to *.
Next row: K to last 2 sts, m1, k1, m1, k1. *(39 sts)*
Next row: P.
Next row: K to last 5 sts, [k2tog] twice, k1. *(37 sts)*
Next row: P.
Rep last 2 rows once more. *(35 sts)*
Next row: K8, turn, work on these 8 sts only, leaving rem sts on needle.
Next row: P2tog, p to end. *(7 sts)*
Next row: K.
Next row: P2tog, p to end. *(6 sts)*
Beg with a k row, work 6 rows in st st.
Bind (cast) off.
Rejoin yarn to rem 27 sts on RS of work.
Next row: Bind (cast) off 16 sts, k to last 3 sts, k2tog, k1. *(10 sts)*
Next row: P2tog, p to last 2 sts, p2tog. *(8 sts)*
Next row: K.
Next row: P2tog, p to last 2 sts, p2tog. *(6 sts)*
Beg with a k row, work 8 rows in st st.
Bind (cast) off.

TAIL

Cast on 12 sts.

Beg with a k row, work 8 rows in st st.

Row 9: K1, k2tog, k to last 3 sts, ssk, k1. *(10 sts)*

Beg with a p row, work 5 rows in st st.

Rep rows 9–14 (last 6 rows) once more. *(8 sts)*

Row 21: K1, k2tog, k to last 2 sts, ssk, k1. *(6 sts)*

Beg with a p row, work 3 rows in st st.

Row 25: K1, k2tog, ssk, k1. *(4 sts)*

Row 26: [P2tog] twice. *(2 sts)*

Row 27: K2tog. *(1 st)*

Fasten off.

EARS

(make 4)

Cast on 5 sts.

Beg with a k row, work 8 rows in st st.

Row 9: Ssk, k1, k2tog. *(3 sts)*

Row 10: P3tog. *(1 st)*

Fasten off.

Making up and finishing

Fold the gusset piece in half lengthwise and mark each end of the fold with a stitch marker or small safety pin. This will mark the center line of the gusset—one half will be sewn to one side of the lower part of the body; the other half will be sewn to the second side of the body. Pin the gusset in position, so the right sides of your work are together. Oversew (see page 91) in place.

Oversew the remaining parts of the body together, leaving a gap in the top for turning and stuffing. Turn and stuff. Stitch the gap closed.

Sew the long seam of the tail using mattress stitch (see page 92). Stuff lightly and oversew in position.

Place two ear pieces right sides together and oversew around the curved edges, leaving lower edges open. Repeat for the second ear. Turn the ears the right way out and sew in position, using the photograph as a guide.

Using black yarn, work two French knots (see page 93) for the eye centers. Using a separated strand of white yarn, work a few coils of chain stitch (see page 93) around each eye center.

Weave in all loose ends.

CHAPTER 3
Bits and Bobs

YARN AND OTHER MATERIALS

Debbie Bliss Rialto DK (100% merino wool; 115yd/105m per 1¾oz/50g ball) light worsted (DK) yarn

  1 ball each of shades:
  12 Scarlet (A)
  65 Pale Pink (B)
  85 Lilac (C)

6yd/5.5m of yarn B for the cord

Approx. ¾oz (20g) 100% polyester toy filling

NEEDLES AND EQUIPMENT

Size US 5 (3.75mm) knitting needles

Yarn sewing needle

GAUGE (TENSION)

24 sts and 40 rows in garter stitch to a 4-in (10-cm) square on US 5 (3.75mm) needles.

MEASUREMENTS

Each heart measures approx. 3in (8cm) tall and 2½in (6cm) wide. The finished garland measures approx. 1¾yd (1.6m).

ABBREVIATIONS

approx.	approximately
inc	increase
k	knit
k2tog	knit two stitches together
m1	make one stitch
psso	pass a slipped stitch over another stitch
rem	remain(ing)
RS	right side(s)
sl1	slip one stitch from the left-hand needle to the right-hand needle without knitting it
ssk	slip one stitch, slip one stitch, knit slipped stitches together
st(s)	stitch(es)
[ ]	work instructions within square brackets as directed

Heart Garland

A knitted garland of pink and red hearts is a romantic new take on traditional bunting. The hearts are knitted entirely in garter stitch and involve only a small amount of shaping—which makes this a great project for the new or intermediate knitter. And as exact size isn't essential for this project, you could use pretty much any light worsted (DK) yarn you have in your stash.

Tip

You can easily make the garland
longer or shorter by knitting more
or fewer hearts and varying the
length of the cord.

Heart

(make three hearts in yarn A, three in B, and three in C)

FRONT/BACK
(make 2 the same)
Cast on 2 sts in A, B, or C.
Row 1: [Inc1] twice. (*4 sts*)
K 3 rows.
Row 5: K1, m1, k2, m1, k1. (*6 sts*)
K 3 rows.
Row 9: K1, m1, k to last st, m1, k1. (*8 sts*)
K 3 rows.
Rep last 4 rows three times more. (*14 sts*)
K 4 rows.
Row 29: K7, turn work.
Row 30: K7.
Row 31: K2tog, k3, ssk. (*5 sts*)
Row 32: K2tog, k1, ssk. (*3 sts*)
Row 33: Sl1, k2tog, psso. (*1 st*)
Break yarn and pull through rem st.
Rejoin yarn to center of work.
K 2 rows.
Row 31: K2tog, k3, ssk. (*5 sts*)
Row 32: K2tog, k1, ssk. (*3 sts*)
Row 33: Sl1, k2tog, psso. (*1 st*)
Break yarn and pull through rem st.

Making up and finishing

Place two matching heart pieces RS together and
oversew (see page 91) round the edges with matching
yarn, leaving a 1-in (2.5-cm) gap at one side for turning
and stuffing. Turn the heart the RS out, stuff lightly, and
stitch the gap closed.

Cut three 2-yd (1.8-m) lengths of B. Knot the three
lengths together at one end and make a 1¾-yd (1.6-m)
braid (plait). Thread the unknotted length of the braided
(plaited) cord through the top of the hearts, alternating
the three colors. Knot the end and distribute the hearts
evenly along the cord, leaving enough cord at each end
to hang the garland up.

Woodland Key Rings

Conjure up a fairytale key ring in virtually no time—you can buy split key rings from most craft stores and the only other items you need are scraps of yarn and the odd button. And because these makes are so small and quick to knit, you can feel free to experiment with other yarns.

YARN AND OTHER MATERIALS

Debbie Bliss Rialto DK (100% merino wool; 115yd/105m per 1¾oz/50g ball) light worsted (DK) yarn
    1 part ball of shade 12 Scarlet (A)
    Very small amounts of 06 Stone (B) (light beige) and 09 Apple (C)
    1 part ball of shade 66 Vintage Pink (D)

Standard white and cream sewing thread

Small amount of 100% polyester toy filling

7 tiny white buttons

1 x ⅝-in (1.5-cm) red button

Split key rings

NEEDLES AND EQUIPMENT

Size US 3 (3.25mm) knitting needles

Yarn sewing needle

Standard sewing needle

GAUGE (TENSION)

24 sts and 32 rows in stockinette (stocking) stitch to a 4-in (10-cm) square on US 3 (3.25mm) needles.

MEASUREMENTS

The toadstool measures 2½in (6cm) in diameter.

The flower measures 2¼in (5.5cm) in diameter.

ABBREVIATIONS

beg	begin(ning)
inc	increase
k	knit
k2tog	knit two stitches together
p2tog	purl two stitches together
rem	remain(ing)
RS	right side(s)
ssk	slip one stitch, slip one stitch, knit slipped stitches together
st(s)	stitch(es)
st st	stockinette (stocking) stitch
WS	wrong side(s)
yo	yarnover
[ ]	work instructions within square brackets as directed

Toadstool

CAP

(make 1)
Cast on 48 sts in A.
Work 7 rows in st st beg with a k row.
Row 8: [P2tog] to end. (*24 sts*)
Row 9: K.
Row 10: [P2tog] to end. (*12 sts*)
Break yarn, thread through rem sts, pull up tightly, and secure.

STALK AND GILLS

(make 1)
Cast on 48 sts in B.
Row 1: K.
Row 2: [P2tog] to end. (*24 sts*)
Row 3: K.
Row 4: [P2tog] to end. (*12 sts*)
Work 10 rows in st st beg with a k row.
Bind (cast) off.

HANGING CORD

(make 1)
Cast on 24 sts in C.
Bind (cast) off.

Making up and finishing

Fold the toadstool cap in half widthwise with RS together and oversew the back seam using A. Fold the stalk and gills in half widthwise with RS together and oversew the lower and back seam using B. Turn both pieces RS out. Oversew (see page 91) the outer edge of gill section to underside of cap, just inside from edge, leaving a gap for stuffing. Stuff quite firmly and sew the gap closed. Using white thread, sew white buttons onto the cap. Sew the hanging cord in place and thread the free end onto the split key ring.

Flower

PETALS

(make 1)
Cast on 60 sts in D.
Work 6 rows in st st.
Row 7: K2, [yo twice, k2tog twice] to last 2 sts, yo twice, k2. (*62 sts*)
Row 8: P.
Row 9: K1, [yo, k2tog] to last st, yo, k1. (*63 sts*)
Work 5 rows in st st beg with a p row.
Bind (cast) off.

LEAVES

(make 2)
Cast on 2 sts in C.
Row 1: [Inc1] twice. (*4 sts*)
Row 2: P.
Row 3: Inc1, k1, inc1, k1. (*6 sts*)
Work 7 rows in st st beg with a p row.
Row 11: K2tog, k2, ssk. (*4 sts*)
Row 12: P.
Row 13: K2tog, ssk. (*2 sts*)
Row 14: P2tog. (*1 st*)
Break yarn and pull through rem st.

HANGING CORD

(make 1)
Cast on 24 sts in A.
Bind (cast) off.

Making up and finishing

Fold the leaf pieces in half widthwise with WS together and oversew (see page 91) round edges using C. Fold the petal strip in half lengthwise with WS together so holes along the middle form a wavy edge. Oversew along lower edge using D. Fold back 1in (2.5cm) along one short edge of petal piece and oversew along bottom. Fold the remainder of the petal strip around the folded part, oversewing in place as you go. Sew the leaves in place. Using cream thread, sew the button in the center of the flower. Sew the hanging cord in place and thread the free end onto the split key ring.

Pencil Case

Create a unique knitted case for your prized writing implements—it is very straightforward to knit although you will need to sew a lining and embroider a few wooly flowers as well. Of course, it doesn't have to be a pencil case—it will also work brilliantly as a make-up bag or just a simple case for keeping all those odds and ends together.

YARN AND OTHER MATERIALS

Sirdar Country Style DK (40% nylon, 30% wool, 30% acrylic; 170yd/155m170yd/155m per 1¾oz/50g ball) light worsted (DK) yarn
   1 ball of shade 654 Saffron (A)

Very small amounts of bright pink, mid-pink, and turquoise light worsted (DK) yarns

3 small buttons in white, pale pink, and pale blue

11 x 9in (28 x 22cm) cotton lining fabric

Standard white and ocher sewing threads

7in (18cm) polyester zipper

NEEDLES AND EQUIPMENT

Size US 8 (5mm) knitting needles

Yarn sewing needle

Large-eyed embroidery needle

Standard sewing needle

GAUGE (TENSION)

17 sts and 25 rows in stockinette (stocking) stitch to a 4-in (10-cm) square on US 8 (5mm) needles, using yarn double.

MEASUREMENTS

The pencil case measures 3¼ x 7in (8 x 18cm).

ABBREVIATIONS

beg	begin(ning)
k	knit
inc	increase
p	purl
rep	repeat
RS	right side(s)
st(s)	stitch(es)
st st	stockinette (stocking) stitch
WS	wrong side(s)

Case

(make 2 the same)
Cast on 32 sts in A, using yarn double.
Work 4 rows in st st beg with a k row.
Row 5: Inc1, k to last 2 sts, inc1, k1. (*34 sts*)
Work 3 rows in st st beg with a p row.
Rep last 4 rows 3 times more. (*40 sts*)
Bind (cast) off.

Making up and finishing

Embroider the flowers on one case piece using lazy daisy stitch (see page 93). Add the button centers, using white thread.

Use one knitted piece as a pattern to cut two lining pieces in cotton fabric, adding an extra ⅜in (1cm) all round for the seams.

Hand stitch the zipper in place between the top edges of both knitted pieces of the case using a double strand of ochre sewing thread.

With WS together, join the side and lower seams using mattress stitch (see page 92) and A.

LINING

Place the two cotton lining pieces RS together and sew round the two short sides and one long side by hand or machine, using a ⅜-in (1-cm) seam allowance. Turn under ⅜ in (1cm) round the top edge. Insert the lining into the pencil case so WS of lining and case are together, and slip stitch in place along the zipper sides.

Cut a few short strands of contrast color yarn and thread through the hole in the zipper pull. Use another short length of the same yarn to tie the strands together to form a tassel.

Tablet Cozy

Keep your treasured tablet safe and sound in its own stripy home. This is one of the simplest projects in the book to knit, and an ideal second or third project for the newbie knitter. As a bonus, it is also very straightforward to seam together. And if you've got small amounts of the same yarn in different shades, why not just make this in stripes of all the colors?

YARN AND OTHER MATERIALS

Schachenmayr Merino Extrafine 120 (100% wool; 131yd/120m per 1¾oz/50g ball) light worsted (DK) yarn
   1 ball each of shades:
   137 Pink (A)
   175 Limone (B) (pale green)

1 x 1-in (25-mm) green button

NEEDLES AND EQUIPMENT

Size US 8 (5mm) knitting needles

Yarn sewing needle

GAUGE (TENSION)

15 sts and 24 rows in stockinette (stocking) stitch to a 4-in (10-cm) square on US 8 (5mm) needles, using yarn double.

MEASUREMENTS

Laid flat the case measures 7¾ x 10in (19.5 x 25cm), to fit a tablet measuring approx. 7¼ x 9½in (18.5 x 24cm). The case will fit the tablet quite snugly, which will help keep it secure.

ABBREVIATIONS

approx.	approximately
beg	begin(ning)
k	knit
k2tog	knit two stitches together
kwise	knitwise
p	purl
rep	repeat
ssk	slip one stitch, slip one stitch, knit slipped stitches together
st(s)	stitch(es)
st st	stockinette (stocking) stitch
WS	wrong side(s)
[ ]	work instructions within square brackets as directed

Cozy

FRONT/BACK
(make 2 the same)
Cast on 32 sts in A, using yarn double.
Rows 1–6: Work in st st beg with a k row.
Leaving A at side, join in a doubled strand of B.
Rows 7–8: Work in st st beg with a k row.
Rep last 8 rows 5 times more.
Fasten off B.
Work 2 rows in st st using A.
Row 51: [K2, p2] to end.
Rep last row twice more.
Bind (cast) off kwise.

FLAP
Cast on 32 sts in A, using yarn double.
Row 1: K.
Row 2: K3, p to last 3 sts, k3.
Rep last 2 rows 3 times more.
Row 9: K1, k2tog, k to last 3 sts, ssk, k1. (*30 sts*)
Row 10: K3, p to last 3 sts, k3.
Row 11: K.
Row 12: K3, p to last 3 sts, k3.
Row 13: K1, k2tog, k to last 3 sts, ssk, k1. (*28 sts*)
Row 14: K1, k2tog, k9, bind (cast) off 4 sts (for the buttonhole), k to last 3 sts, ssk, k1. (*22 sts*)
Row 15: K1, k2tog, k8, turn work and cast on 4 sts (for the buttonhole), turn work again, k to last 3 sts, ssk, k1. (*24 sts*)
Row 16: K1, k2tog, k to last 3 sts, ssk, k1. (*22 sts*)
Bind (cast) off.

Making up and finishing

With WS together, join the front and back of the cozy together at the sides using mattress stitch (see page 92) and A. Oversew (see page 91) the lower seam from the inside. From the outside, oversew the flap in place along the top of the back.

Sew the button in place using a separated strand of B.

Phone Cozy

This cozy can also be used to protect your phone when you're on the go. It's designed to fit snugly and there are no fiddly fastenings to undo so you won't miss important calls. The simple cable pattern makes it a great project to take that first step up from plain and purl knitting. You can use up your leftover light worsted (DK) yarns for this project, and cast on more or fewer stitches at the beginning and end of each row if necessary to fit your phone.

YARN AND OTHER MATERIALS

Patons Diploma Gold DK (55% wool, 25% acrylic, 20% nylon; 131yd/120m per 1¾oz/50g ball) light worsted (DK) yarn
    1 ball of shade 6136 Denim

NEEDLES AND EQUIPMENT

Size US 3 (3.25mm) knitting needles

Small or medium cable needle

Yarn sewing needle

GAUGE (TENSION)

24 sts and 36 rows in stockinette (stocking) stitch to a 4-in (10-cm) square on US 3 (3.25mm) needles.

MEASUREMENTS

To fit a phone approx. 4¾ –5in (12–12.5cm) high and 2½in (6.5cm) wide.

NOTE

If you are adapting the pattern for a different size of phone, add or subtract an even number of stitches and keep the cable central.

ABBREVIATIONS

approx.	approximately
k	knit
p	purl
rep	repeat
RS	right side
st(s)	stitch(es)
tbl	through back loop (work through the back loop of the stitch only)
[ ]	work instructions within square brackets as directed

Cozy

FRONT/BACK
(make 2 the same)
Cast on 19 sts.
Row 1: P6, k1, [p1, k1] 3 times, p6.
Row 2: K6, p1tbl, [k1, p1tbl] 3 times, k6.
Rep last 2 rows once more.
Row 5: P6, slip next 4 sts onto cable needle and leave at back of work, k1, p1, k1, then p1, k1, p1, k1 from cable needle, p6.
Row 6: K6, p1tbl, [k1, p1tbl] 3 times, k6.
Row 7: P6, k1, [p1, k1] 3 times, p6.
Row 8: K6, p1tbl, [k1, p1tbl] 3 times, k6.
Rep last 2 rows once more.
Rows 11–30: Rep rows 1–10 twice more.
Rows 31–36: Rep rows 1–6 once more.
Row 37: [K1, p1] to last st, k1.
Row 38: [P1, k1] to last st, p1.
Rows 39–40: Rep rows 37–38.
Bind (cast) off keeping to the k1, p1 pattern.

Making up and finishing

Join the two side seams using flat stitch (see page 91). With the cozy RS together, oversew (see page 91) the bottom seam. Turn the cozy RS out.

Wallet

If you're fed up with all those boring wallets out there, why not give your money and bank cards a treat and knit them their own cozy home? This cute case is knitted in a firm textured stitch in a smooth, soft yarn. It has two pockets for cards and a separate pocket for bank notes. We've brightened our wallet up with a bright pink button but, of course, the color choices are up to you.

YARN AND OTHER MATERIALS

Sirdar Country Style DK (40% nylon, 30% wool, 30% acrylic; 170yd/155m per 1¾oz/50g ball) light worsted (DK) yarn

> 1 ball each of shades:
> 389 Smokey Stone (A) (pale green)
> 409 Naturelle (B) (blush pink)

1 x ¾-in (2-cm) bright pink button

1 x ⅝-in (1.5-cm) snap fastener

Standard cream sewing thread

NEEDLES AND EQUIPMENT

Size US 2/3 (3mm) knitting needles

Yarn sewing needle

Standard sewing needle

GAUGE (TENSION)

25 sts and 28 rows over main pattern on outer part of wallet to a 4-in (10-cm) square on US 2/3 (3mm) needles.

MEASUREMENTS

The wallet measures 4 x 5½in (10 x 14cm) when closed.

ABBREVIATIONS

beg	begin(ning)
k	knit
k2tog	knit two stitches together
p	purl
rep	repeat
RS	right side(s)
ssk	slip one stitch, slip one stitch, knit slipped stitches together
st(s)	stitch(es)
st st	stockinette (stocking) stitch
[ ]	work instructions within square brackets as directed

Wallet

OUTER WALLET
(make 1)
Cast on 35 sts in A.
K 2 rows.
Row 3: K2, p to last 2 sts, k2.
Row 4: K5, p1, [k5, p1] to last 5 sts, k5.
Row 5: K2, p2, k1, p1, k1, [p3, k1, p1, k1] to last 4 sts, p2, k2.
Row 6: K3, p1, [k3, p1, k1, p1] to last 7 sts, k3, p1, k3.
Row 7: K3, [p5, k1] to last 2 sts, k2.
Row 8: K3, p1, [k3, p1, k1, p1] to last 7 sts, k3, p1, k3.
Row 9: K2, p2, k1, p1, k1, [p3, k1, p1, k1] to last 4 sts, p2, k2.
Rep last 6 rows 5 times more.
Row 40: K5, p1, [k5, p1] to last 5 sts, k5.
K 5 rows.
Row 46: K5, p1, [k5, p1] to last 5 sts, k5.
Row 47: K2, p2, k1, p1, k1, [p3, k1, p1, k1] to last 4 sts, p2, k2.
Row 48: K3, p1, [k3, p1, k1, p1] to last 7 sts, k3, p1, k3.
Row 49: K3, [p5, k1] to last 2 sts, k2.
Row 50: K3, p1, [k3, p1, k1, p1] to last 7 sts, k3, p1, k3.
Row 51: K2, p2, k1, p1, k1, [p3, k1, p1, k1] to last 4 sts, p2, k2.
Rep last 6 rows 5 times more.
Row 82: K5, p1, [k5, p1] to last 5 sts, k5.
K 2 rows.
Bind (cast) off.

LINING
(make 1)

The lining is knitted from the card pocket edge to the note pocket edge.

Cast on 34 sts in B.

K2 rows.

Work 17 rows in st st beg with a k row.

Now begin with a k row to work the RS of st st on the other side.

Work 31 rows in st st beg with a k row.

K 5 rows.

Work 35 rows in st st beg with a k row.

Now begin with a k row to work the RS of st st on the other side.

Work 23 rows in st st beg with a k row.

K 2 rows.

Bind (cast) off.

CLOSURE
(make 1)

Cast on 12 sts in A.

Row 1: K.

Row 2: K2, p to last 2 sts, k2.

Rep last 2 rows 7 times more.

Row 17: K.

Row 18: K2tog, k to last 2 sts, ssk.

Bind (cast) off 10 sts.

Making up and finishing

Fold the two sides of the lining toward the center to form the two pocket sections and oversew (see page 91) at the sides, very close to the edge. Work a line of chain stitch (see page 93) along the center of the card pocket to form two equal sections.

Oversew the lining to the outer wallet, making sure the central garter stitch columns line up. The lining should be sewn just inside the outer edge of the outer wallet.

Oversew the closure in position on the underside of the wallet. Sew one half of the snap fastener on the underside of the closure and the other half to match to it on the top face of the wallet. Sew the button on the outside of the closure.

YARN AND OTHER MATERIALS

Sirdar Country Style DK (40% nylon, 30% wool, 30% acrylic; 170yd/155m per 1¾oz/50g ball) light worsted (DK) yarn
  1 ball of shade 409 Naturelle (A)

Very small amounts of any light worsted (DK) yarn in each of shades:
  Mid-blue (B)
  Dark red (C)
  Dark gray (D)

2 x 4in (5 x 10cm) rectangle of plain white or cream cheesecloth or fine cotton

¼–½oz (10g) 100% polyester toy filling

Small handful of dried lavender

NEEDLES AND EQUIPMENT

Size US 3 (3.25mm) knitting needles

Yarn sewing needle

Large-eyed embroidery needle

Standard sewing needle and white or cream sewing thread

GAUGE (TENSION)

24 sts and 32 rows in stockinette (stocking) stitch to a 4-in (10-cm) square on US 3 (3.25mm) needles.

MEASUREMENTS

The owl is approx. 4in (10cm) tall.

ABBREVIATIONS

approx.	approximately
inc	increase
k	knit
k2tog	knit two stitches together
kwise	knitwise
m1	make one stitch
p	purl
rep	repeat
ssk	slip one stitch, slip one stitch, knit slipped stitches together
st(s)	stitch(es)
st st	stockinette (stocking) stitch
WS	wrong side(s)
*	work instructions after/between asterisk(s) as directed.

Owl Lavender Bag

This wise little owl, with his simple textured front, will keep your linens smelling floral-fresh or would make an excellent stocking filler or small gift. Tuck it among your small clothing items or add a loop of ribbon if you want your ornithological lavender bag to adorn a coat hanger.

Owl

BACK

(make 1)

Cast on 14 sts in A.

Row 1: Inc1, k to last 2 sts, inc1, k1. (*16 sts*)
Row 2: P.
Row 3: K2, M1, k to last 2 sts, m1, k1. (*18 sts*)
Row 4: P.
Rep last 2 rows once more. (20 sts)*
Work 20 rows in st st beg with a k row.
Row 27: K2, k2tog, k to last 4 sts, ssk, k2. (*18 sts*)
Work 3 rows in st st beg with a p row.
Row 31: K2, k2tog, k to last 4 sts, ssk, k2. (*16 sts*)
Row 32: P.
Row 33: K2, k2tog, k to last 4 sts, ssk, k2. (*14 sts*)
Row 34: K.
Row 35: K2, m1, k to last 2 sts, m1, k2. (*16 sts*)
Bind (cast) off kwise.

FRONT

(make 1)

Work as for back until *.
Row 7: K7, p6, k7.
Row 8: P.
Row 9: K6, p8, k6.
Row 10: P.
Row 11: K5, p10, k5.
Row 12: P.
Rep last 2 rows 3 times more.
Row 19: K6, p8, k6.
Row 20: P.
Row 21: K7, p6, k7.
Row 22: P.
Row 23: K8, p4, k8.
Work 3 rows in st st beg with a p row.
Row 27: K2, k2tog, k to last 4 sts, ssk, k2. (*18 sts*)
Work 3 rows in st st beg with a p row.
Row 31: K2, k2tog, k to last 4 sts, ssk, k2. (*16 sts*)
Row 32: P.
Row 33: K2, k2tog, k to last 4 sts, ssk, k2. (*14 sts*)
Row 34: K.
Row 35: K2, m1, k to last 2 sts, m1, k2. (*16 sts*)
Bind (cast) off kwise.

Making up and finishing

With back and front WS together, join the sides of the owl using mattress stitch (see page 92) , leaving a gap at the side for stuffing. Oversew (see page 91) the lower seam from the inside and the top seam from the outside.

Fold the rectangle of fabric in half widthwise and sew the two side seams. Fill with lavender and then stitch the top closed.

Stuff the owl with fiberfill, inserting the lavender bag inside, then stitch the gap closed.

Using B, work two sets of lazy daisy stitch (see page 93) for the eyes. Using C, work a French knot (see page 93) in the center of each eye for the pupil. Using D, work two sets of straight stitch (seee page 93), one over the other, to form a V-shape for the beak.

techniques

On the following pages you'll find the basic knitting techniques that you will need for the patterns in this book.

gauge (tension)

The gauge (tension) is given as the number of stitches and rows needed to produce a 4-in (10-cm) square of knitting.

Using the recommended yarn and needles, cast on 8 stitches more than the gauge (tension) instruction asks for. Working in pattern, work 8 rows more than needed. Bind (cast) off loosely. Lay the swatch flat without stretching it. Lay a ruler across the stitches with the 2in (5cm) mark centered on the knitting, then put a pin in the knitting at the 0 and at the 4in (10cm) mark. Count the number of stitches between the pins. Repeat the process across the rows to count the number of rows to 4in (10cm).

If the number of stitches and rows you've counted is the same as the number asked for, you have the correct gauge (tension). If you do not have the same number then you will need to change your gauge (tension) by changing

the size of your knitting needles. A good rule of thumb is that one difference in needle size will create a difference of one stitch in the gauge (tension). Use larger needles to achieve fewer stitches and smaller ones to achieve more stitches.

If you are knitting in a different yarn to that suggested in the pattern, you may need to knit on thinner or thicker needles than stated on the yarn's ball band to achieve the right tension (see Substituting yarn, opposite).

holding needles

If you are a knitting novice, you will need to discover which is the most comfortable way for you to hold your needles.

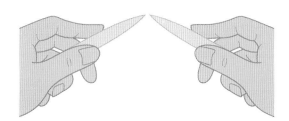

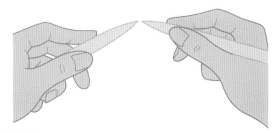

LIKE A KNIFE

Pick up the needles, one in each hand, as if you were holding a knife and fork—that is to say, with your hands lightly over the top of each needle. As you knit, you will tuck the blunt end of the right-hand needle under your arm, let go with your hand, and use your hand to manipulate the yarn, returning your hand to the needle to move the stitches along.

LIKE A PEN

Now try changing the right hand so you are holding the needle as you would hold a pen, with your thumb and forefinger lightly gripping the needle close to its pointed tip and the shaft resting in the crook of your thumb. As you knit, you will not need to let go of the needle but simply slide your right hand forward to manipulate the yarn.

holding yarn

As you knit, you work stitches off the left-hand needle onto the right-hand needle, and the yarn needs to be held and tensioned to produce even fabric. Use either your right or left hand, depending on the method you use to make stitches.

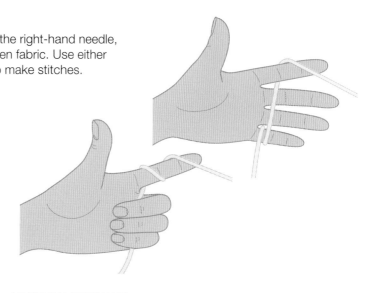

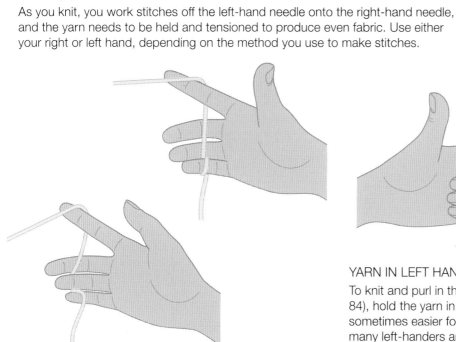

YARN IN RIGHT HAND

To knit and purl in the US/UK style (see pages 83 and 84), hold the yarn in your right hand. You can wind the yarn around your fingers in different ways, depending on how tightly you need to hold it to achieve an even gauge (tension). Try both ways shown to find out which works best for you.

To hold the yarn tightly (top right), wind it right around your little finger, under your ring and middle fingers, then pass it over your index finger, which will manipulate the yarn.

For a looser hold (below right), catch the yarn between your little and ring fingers, pass it under your middle finger, then over your index finger.

YARN IN LEFT HAND

To knit and purl in the Continental style (see pages 83 and 84), hold the yarn in your left hand. This method is sometimes easier for left-handed people to use, though many left-handers are quite comfortable knitting with the yarn in their right hand. Try the ways shown to find out which works best for you.

To hold the yarn tightly (top right), wind it right around your little finger, under your ring and middle fingers, then pass it over your index finger, which will manipulate the yarn.

For a looser hold (below left), fold your little, ring, and middle fingers over the yarn, and wind it twice around your index finger.

substituting yarn

Each pattern includes either the yarn used or a suggested weight where an exact match isn't crucial.

Information on fiber content, weight and length per ball, and gauge (tension) are all included in the pattern; if you want to use a different yarn from your stash, try and match these elements as closely as possible, but in some cases an exact gauge (tension) match may not be possible. That won't matter for some makes, where exact size isn't crucial, or where the make is very small.

And as you already have the yarn, it is worth experimenting a bit with different sized needles, and perhaps knitting a few more rows if needed, to get the right result.

knitting with yarn doubled

Some of the patterns will tell you to knit with two strands of yarn at the same time (doubled). Where you are using two strands of the same yarn and you only have one ball of it, you can take one end from the outside of the ball, and the other end from inside the middle of the ball. Take care to pick up each strand as you knit or purl into them together.

making a slip knot

You will need to make a slip knot to form your first cast-on stitch.

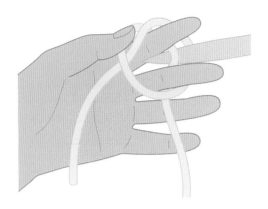 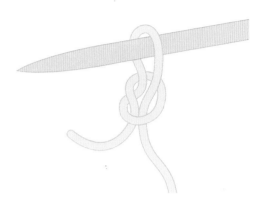

1 With the ball of yarn on your right, lay the end of the yarn on the palm of your left hand and hold it in place with your left thumb. With your right hand, take the yarn around your top two fingers to form a loop. Take the knitting needle through the back of the loop from right to left and use it to pick up the strand nearest to the yarn ball, as shown in the diagram. Pull the strand through to form a loop at the front.

2 Slip the yarn off your fingers, leaving the loop on the needle. Gently pull on both yarn ends to tighten the knot. Then pull on the yarn leading to the ball of yarn to tighten the knot on the needle.

casting on (cable method)

There are a few methods of casting on but the one used for the projects in this book is the cable method, which uses two needles.

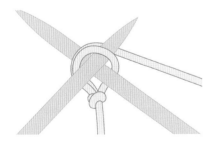  

1 Make a slip knot as shown above. Put the needle with the slip knot into your left hand. Insert the point of the other needle into the front of the slip knot and under the left-hand needle. Wind the yarn from the ball of yarn around the tip of the right-hand needle.

2 Using the tip of the needle, draw the yarn through the slip knot to form a loop. This loop is the new stitch. Slip the loop from the right-hand needle onto the left-hand needle.

3 To make the next stitch, insert the tip of the right-hand needle between the two stitches. Wind the yarn over the right-hand needle, from left to right, then draw the yarn through to form a loop. Transfer this loop to the left-hand needle. Repeat until you have cast on the right number of stitches for the project.

knit stitch

There are only two stitches to master in knitting; knit stitch and purl stitch. Most people in the English-speaking world knit using a method called English (or American) knitting. However, in parts of Europe, people prefer a method known as Continental knitting.

US/UK STYLE

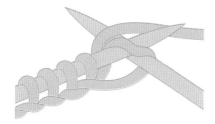 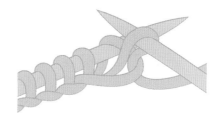 

1 Hold the needle with the cast-on stitches in your left hand, and then insert the point of the right-hand needle into the front of the first stitch from left to right. Wind the yarn around the point of the right-hand needle, from left to right.

2 With the tip of the right-hand needle, pull the yarn through the stitch to form a loop. This loop is the new stitch.

3 Slip the original stitch off the left-hand needle by gently pulling the right-hand needle to the right. Repeat these steps till you have knitted all the stitches on the left-hand needle. To work the next row, transfer the needle with all the stitches into your left hand.

CONTINENTAL STYLE

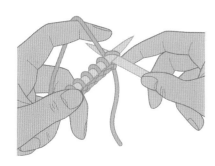 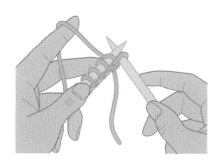 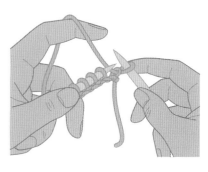

1 Hold the needle with the stitches to be knitted in your left hand, and then insert the tip of the right-hand needle into the front of the first stitch from left to right. Holding the yarn fairly taut with your left hand at the back of your work, use the tip of the right-hand needle to pick up a loop of yarn.

2 With the tip of the right-hand needle, bring the yarn through the original stitch to form a loop. This loop is the new stitch.

3 Slip the original stitch off the left-hand needle by gently pulling the right-hand needle to the right. Repeat these steps till you have knitted all the stitches on the left-hand needle. To work the next row, transfer the needle with all the stitches into your left hand.

purl stitch

As with knit stitch, purl stitch can be formed in two ways. If you are new to knitting, try both techniques to see which works better for you: left-handed people may find the Continental method easier to master.

CONTINENTAL STYLE

US/UK STYLE

1 Hold the needle with the stitches in your left hand, and then insert the point of the right-hand needle into the front of the first stitch from right to left. Wind the yarn around the point of the right-hand needle, from right to left.

2 With the tip of the right-hand needle, pull the yarn through the stitch to form a loop. This loop is the new stitch.

1 Hold the needle with the stitches to be knitted in your left hand, and then insert the tip of the right-hand needle into the front of the first stitch from right to left. Holding the yarn fairly taut at the front of the work, move the tip of the right-hand needle under the working yarn, then push your left index finger downward, as shown, to hold the yarn around the needle.

3 Slip the original stitch off the left-hand needle by gently pulling the right-hand needle to the right. Repeat these steps till you have purled all the stitches on the left-hand needle. To work the next row, transfer the needle with all the stitches into your left hand.

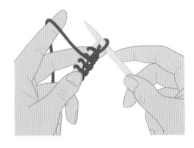

2 With the tip of the right-hand needle, bring the yarn through the original stitch to form a loop.

binding (casting) off

You need to bind (cast) off the stitches to complete the projects and stop the knitting unraveling.

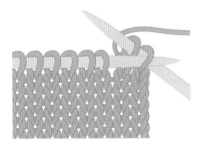

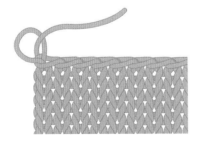

1 First knit two stitches in the normal way. With the point of the left-hand needle, pick up the first stitch you have just knitted and lift it over the second stitch. Knit another stitch so that there are two stitches on the right-hand needle again. Repeat the process of lifting the first stitch over the second stitch. Continue this process until there is just one stitch remaining on the right-hand needle.

2 Break the yarn, leaving a tail of yarn long enough to sew the work together (see page 91). Pull the tail all the way through the last stitch. Slip the stitch off the needle and pull it fairly tightly to make sure it is secure.

3 Slip the original stitch off the left-hand needle by gently pulling the right-hand needle to the right. Repeat these steps till you have purled all the stitches on the left-hand needle. To work the next row, transfer the needle with all the stitches into your left hand.

picking up stitches

For some projects, you will need to pick up stitches along either a horizontal edge (the cast-on or bound-/cast-off edge of your knitting), or a vertical edge (the edges of your rows of knitting).

ALONG A ROW-END EDGE

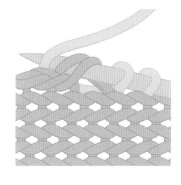

With the right side of the knitting facing you, insert a knitting needle from the front to back between the first and second stitches of the first row. Wind the yarn around the needle and pull through a loop to form the new stitch. Normally you have more gaps between rows than stitches you need to pick up and knit. To make sure your picking up is even, you will have to miss a gap every few rows.

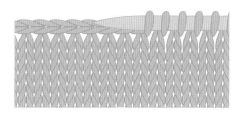

ALONG A CAST-ON OR BOUND- (CAST-) OFF EDGE

This is worked in the same way as picking up stitches along a vertical edge, except that you will work through the cast-on stitches rather than the gaps between rows. You will normally have the same number of stitches to pick up and knit as there are existing stitches.

slipping stitches

This means moving stitches from one needle to the other without knitting or purling them. They can be slipped knitwise or purlwise depending on the row you are working, or any specific pattern instructions.

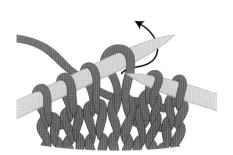

KNITWISE

From left to right, put the right-hand needle into the next stitch on the left-hand needle (as shown by the arrow) and slip it across onto the right-hand needle without working it.

PURLWISE

You can slip a stitch purlwise on a purl row or a knit row. From right to left, put the right-hand needle into the next stitch on the left-hand needle and slip it across onto the right-hand needle without working it.

yarnover (yo)

To make a yarnover, wind the yarn around the right-hand needle to make an extra loop that is worked as a stitch on the next row.

Bring the yarn between the tips of the needles to the front. Take the yarn over the right-hand needle to the back and knit the next stitch on the left-hand needle (see page 93).

through the back loop (tbl)

You usually knit or purl stitches by putting the right-hand needle into the front of the stitch. However, sometimes a stitch needs to be twisted to creat an effect or to work a technique, and to do this you knit or purl into the back of it. This is called "working through the back loop" and is abbreviated to "tbl" in a knitting pattern.

increasing

There are three methods of increasing used in projects in this book.

KNIT TBL

Put the right-hand needle into the back of the next stitch on the left-hand needle. Knit the stitch in the usual way (see page 83), but through the back loop.

PURL TBL

Put the right-hand needle into the back of the next stitch on the left-hand needle (from left to right). Purl the stitch in the usual way (see page 84), but through the back loop.

INCREASE ON A KNIT ROW (inc)

1 Knit the next stitch on the left-hand needle in the usual way (see page 83), but do not slip the "old" stitch off the left-hand needle.

2 Move the right-hand needle behind the left-hand needle and put it into the same stitch again, but through the back of the stitch this time. Knit the stitch again.

INCREASE ON A PURL ROW (inc pwise)

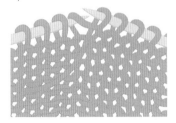

1 Purl the next stitch on the left-hand needle in the usual way (see page 84), but do not slip the "old" stitch off the left-hand needle.

2 Twist the right-hand needle backward to make it easier to put it into the same stitch again, but through the back of the stitch this time. Purl the stitch again, then slip the "old" stitch off the left-hand needle in the usual way.

3 Now slip the "old" stitch off the left-hand needle in the usual way.

MAKE ONE STITCH (m1)

1 From the front, slip the tip of the left-hand needle under the horizontal strand of yarn running between the last stitch on the right-hand needle and the first stitch on the left-hand needle.

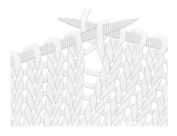

2 Put the right-hand needle knitwise into the back of the loop formed by the picked-up strand and knit into it in the normal way. (It is important to knit into the back of the loop so that it is twisted and a hole does not form in your work.)

decreasing

There are five different ways of decreasing used in this book.

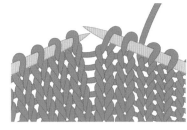

1 Slip one stitch knitwise, and then the next stitch knitwise onto the right-hand needle, without knitting either of them.

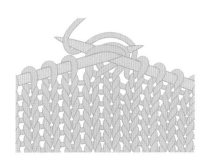

KNIT TWO TOGETHER (k2tog)

This is the simplest way of decreasing. Simply insert the right-hand needle through two stitches instead of the normal one, and then knit them in the usual way.

The same principle is used to knit three stitches together; just insert the right-hand needle through three stitches instead of through two.

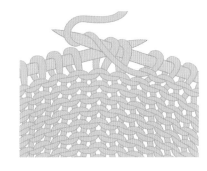

PURL TWO TOGETHER (p2tog)

To make a simple decrease on a purl row, insert the right-hand needle through two stitches instead of the normal one, and then purl them in the usual way (see page 84).

The same principle is used to purl three stitches together; just insert the right-hand needle through three stitches instead of through two.

2 Insert the left-hand needle from left to right through the front loops of both the slipped stitches and knit them in the usual way.

SLIP ONE, KNIT ONE, PASS THE SLIPPED STITCH OVER (sl1,k1, psso)

Slip the first stitch knitwise from the left-hand to the right-hand needle without knitting it (see page 85). Knit the next stitch. Then lift the slipped stitch over the knitted stitch and drop it off the needle.

SLIP TWO, KNIT ONE, PASS SLIPPED STITCHES OVER (sl2, k1,psso)

Slip two stiches knitwise from the left-hand to the right-hand needle without knitting them (see page 85). Knit the next stitch. Then lift both slipped stitches over the knitted stitch and drop them off the needle.

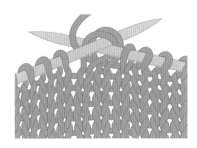

SLIP ONE, KNIT TWO TOGETHER, PASS THE SLIPPED STITCH OVER (sl1,k2tog, psso)

Slip the first stitch knitwise from the left-hand to the right-hand needle without knitting it (see page 85). Knit the next two stitches together (see above). Then lift the slipped stitch over the knitted stitch and drop it off the needle.

cables

This is another technique that looks difficult, but really isn't. All you are doing is moving groups of stitches using a cable needle. Work a six-stitch cable as shown here: if it is a four-stitch cable, then slip two stitches onto the needle and knit two, rather than three.

CABLE SIX FRONT

This cable twists to the left and is abbreviated to "C6F" in a knitting pattern.

 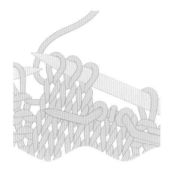 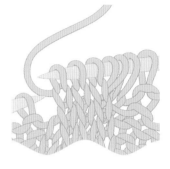

1 Work to the position of the cable. Slip the next three stitches on the left-hand needle purlwise (see page 85) onto the cable needle, then leave the cable needle in front of the work.

2 Knit the next three stitches off the left-hand needle in the usual way (see page 83).

3 Then knit the three stitches off the cable needle. The cable is completed.

CABLE SIX BACK

This cable twists to the right and is abbreviated to "C6B" in a knitting pattern.

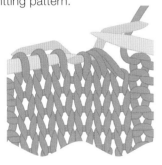 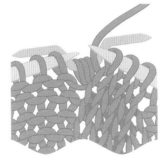 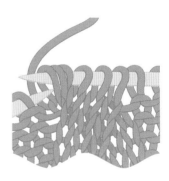

1 Work to the position of the cable. Slip the next three stitches on the left-hand needle purlwise (see page 85) onto the cable needle, then leave the cable needle at the back of the work.

2 Knit the next three stitches of the left-hand needle in the usual way (see page 83).

3 Then knit the three stitches off the cable needle. The cable is completed.

stranding

It's important to change colors in the right way to keep the knitted fabric flat and smooth and without any holes or gaps. If you are knitting just a few stitches in a different color, you can simply leave the color you are not using on the wrong side of the work and pick it up again when you need to.

CHANGING COLOR ON A KNIT ROW

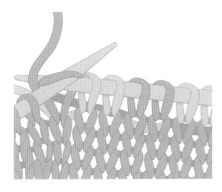

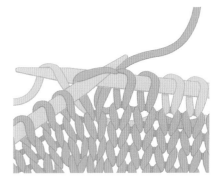

1 Knit the stitches (see page 83) in color A (brown in this example), bringing the yarn across over the strand of color B (lime in this example) to wrap around the needle.

2 At the color change, drop color A and pick up color B, bringing it across under the strand of color A to wrap around the needle. Be careful not to pull it too tight. Knit the stitches in color B. When you change back to color A, bring it across over the strand of color B.

CHANGING COLOR ON A PURL ROW

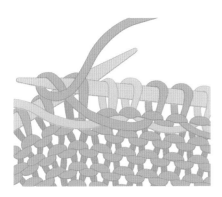

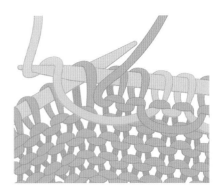

1 Purl the stitches (see page 84) in color A (brown in this example), bringing it across over the strand of color B (lime in this example) to wrap around the needle.

2 At the color change, drop color A and pick up color B, bringing it across under the strand of color A to wrap around the needle. Be careful not to pull it too tight. Purl the stitches in color B. When you change back to color A, bring it across over the strand of color B.

intarsia

If you are knitting blocks of different colors within a project then you will need to use a technique called intarsia. This involves having separate balls of yarn for each area and twisting the yarns together where they join to avoid creating a hole or gap.

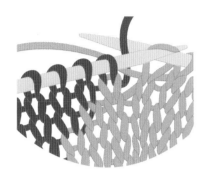
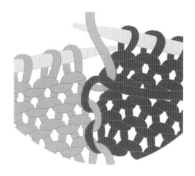

ON THE RIGHT SIDE

When you want to change colors and the color change is vertical or sloping to the right, take the first color over the second color. Then pick up the second color, so the strands of yarn cross each other.

ON THE WRONG SIDE

On this side it is easy to see how the yarns must be interlinked at each color change. This is worked in almost the same way as on the right side. When you want to change colors and the color change is vertical or sloping to the left, take the first color over the second color. Then pick up the second color, so the strands of yarn cross each other.

carrying yarn up the side of the work

When you knit stripe patterns you do not need to join in a new color for every stripe. Instead, carry the color not in use up the side of the work until you need it again.

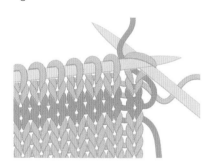
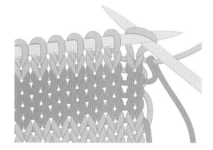

1 If the stripes change every two rows, then just bring the yarn not in use up and knit with it as needed.

2 If the stripes are wider, then you need to catch in the yarn not in use at the ends of rows to prevent long, loose strands appearing. To do this, put the right-hand needle into the first stitch of a row, lay the yarn to be carried over the working yarn, and then knit the stitch in the working yarn.

sewing in ends

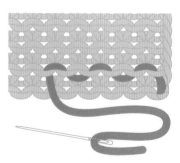

The easiest way to finish yarn ends is to run a few small stitches forward then backward through your work, ideally in a seam. Use a pointed needle because working between the individual strands that make up the yarn can help the yarn tail stay put.

blocking

If, once you have finished the piece of knitting, it doesn't look as smooth and even as you hoped it would, then blocking it can help. You can also use this process to straighten or to re-shape pieces a little if need be. The precise method of blocking you use depends on the fiber the yarn is spun from: the ball band will give you advice on that.

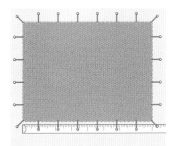

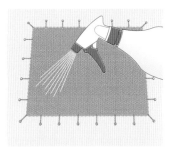

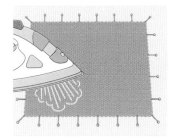

1 Lay the piece of knitting flat on an ironing board and ease it in to shape. Don't pull hard and keep the knitting flat. Starting at the corners (if there are any), pin the edges of the piece to the ironing board, pushing the pins in far enough to hold the knitting firmly. Use a ruler or tape measure to check that the pinned pieces are the right size.

2 If the fiber or texture of your yarn does not respond well to heat, then use a spray bottle of cold water to completely dampen the knitting, but do not make it soaking wet. Leave the knitting to dry naturally, then unpin it.

3 If you can use heat, then set the iron to the temperature the yarn ball band recommends. Hold the iron 1in (2.5cm) above the surface of the knitting and steam it for a couple of minutes. Move the iron so that the whole surface gets steamed, but don't actually touch the knitting with the iron as this can spoil the texture and drape of the fabric and may leave shiny patches. Leave the knitting to dry naturally, then unpin it.

sewing seams

There are various ways of sewing pieces together, and the patterns advise you on which method to use.

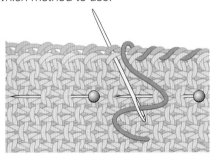

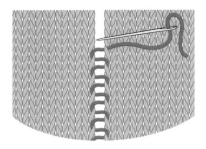

OVERSEWING

This stitch can be worked with the right or the wrong sides of the work together. Thread a yarn sewing needle with a tail left after binding (casting) off, or a long length of yarn. Bring the yarn from the back of the work, over the edge of the knitting, and out through to the back again a short distance further on.

FLAT STITCH

Unlike mattress stitch (see page 92), this creates a seam that is completely flat. Lay the two edges to be joined side by side with the right sides facing you. Using a yarn sewing needle, pick up the very outermost strand of knitting from one side and then the other, working your way along the seam and pulling the yarn up firmly every few stitches.

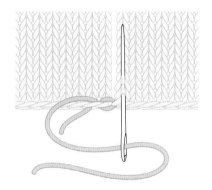

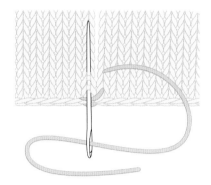

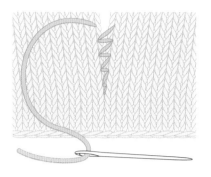

1 Right-sides up, lay the edges to be joined side by side. Thread a yarn sewing needle and from the back, bring it up between the first and second stitches of the left-hand piece, immediately above the cast-on edge. Take it across to the right-hand piece, and from the back bring it through between the first two stitches, immediately above the cast-on edge. Take it back to the left-hand piece and from the back, bring it through where it first came out. Pull the yarn through and this figure-eight will hold the cast-on edges level. Take the needle across to the right-hand piece and, from the front, take it under the bars of yarn between the first and second stitches on the next two rows up.

2 Take the needle across to the left-hand piece and, from the front, take it under the bars of yarn between the first and second stitches on the next two rows up. Continue in this way, taking the needle under two bars on one piece and then the other, to sew up the seam.

3 When you have sewn about 1in (2.5cm), gently and evenly pull the stitches tight to close the seam, and then continue to complete the sewing.

MATTRESS STITCH ON CAST-ON AND BOUND- (CAST-) OFF EDGES

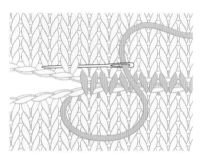

1 Right-sides up, lay the two edges to be joined side by side. Thread a yarn sewing needle with a tail left after binding (casting) off, or a long length of yarn. Secure the yarn on the back of the lower knitted piece, then bring the needle up through the middle of the first whole stitch in that piece. Take the needle under both "legs" of the first whole stitch on the upper piece, so that it comes to the front between the first and second stitches.

2 Go back into the lower piece and take the needle through to the back where it first came out, and then bring it back to the front in the middle of the next stitch along. Pull the yarn through. Take the needle under both "legs" of the next whole stitch on the upper piece. Repeat this step to sew the seam. Pull the stitches gently taut to close the seam as you work.

embroidery stitches

When embroidering on knitting, take the embroidery needle in and out of the work between the strands that make up the yarn rather than between the knitted stitches themselves; this will help make your embroidery look more even.

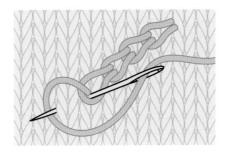

CHAIN STITCH

Bring the yarn out at the starting point on the front of the work. Take the needle back into the knitting just next to the starting point, leaving a loop of yarn. Bring the needle out of the work again, a stitch length further on and catch the loop under it. Pull the thread up firmly, but not so tight that it pulls the knitting. Continue in this way until the stitching is complete.

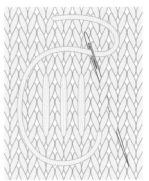

STRAIGHT STITCH

To make this stitch, simply take the yarn out at the starting point and back down into the work where you want the stitch to end.

To work satin stitch, work straight stitches very close together.

FRENCH KNOT

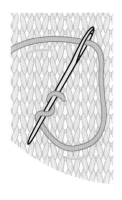

1 Bring the yarn out at the starting point, where you want the French knot to sit. Wind the yarn around the needle twice, or three times for a larger knot.

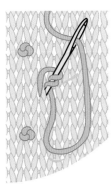

2 Take the needle back into the work, just to the side of the starting point. Gently pull the needle and yarn through the work and slide the knot off the needle and onto the knitting, pulling it taut. Then bring the needle out at the point for the next French knot or, if you are working a single knot, secure it on the back.

LAZY DAISY

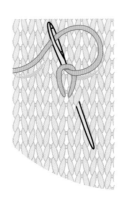

1 Bringing the yarn out where the center of the flower will be, make a single chain stitch (see above), and anchor the loop in place with a tiny straight stitch.

2 Repeat Step 1 to make a daisy flower with as many petals as required.

making pompoms

1 Using either a pair of card rings cut to the size pompom you would like to create, or a pompom maker in the desired size, cut a length of yarn and wind it around the rings until the rings are completely full. You can use more than one color of yarn for a multicolored pompom by using shorter lengths of each color and switching between them.

2 Cut through the loops around the outer edge of the rings and ease them slightly apart. Thread a length of yarn between the layers and tie tightly, leaving a long end. Remove the card rings and fluff up the pompom. Use the long tail to stitch it in place very securely. Trim off the yarn tail and any odd long ends.

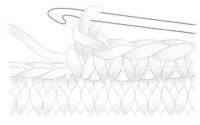

crochet chain

A few projects require a simple crochet chain.

1 Make a slip knot on the crochet hook in the same way as for knitting (see page 82). Holding the slip stitch on the hook, wind the yarn around the hook from the back to the front, then catch the yarn in the crochet-hook tip.

2 Pull the yarn through the slip stitch on the crochet hook to make the second link in the chain. Continue in this way till the chain is the length needed.

crochet edging

1 A crochet edging can be worked along a horizontal edge or a vertical edge, but the basic technique is the same. Insert the crochet hook in the first space between stitches. Wind the yarn round the hook and pull a loop of yarn through.

2 Wind the yarn round the hook again and then pull the loop through to make a single chain.

3 Insert the hook through the next stitch, wind the yarn round the hook, and pull through a second loop of yarn.

4 Wind the yarn round the hook and pull a loop of yarn through both loops on the hook. Repeat steps 3 and 4, inserting the hook into the spaces between stitches in an even pattern.

For crochet edging along a vertical edge, insert your hook into the spaces between the edges of the rows rather than the spaces between stitches.

abbreviations

approx.	approximately		**p2sso**	pass two slipped stitches over
beg	begin(ning)		**pwise**	purlwise
C4F	cable four front		**rem**	remain(ing)
C6B	cable six back		**rep**	repeat
C6F	cable six front		**RH**	right-hand
cm	centimeter(s)		**RS**	right side(s)
cont	continue		**sl1**	slip one stitch from the left-hand needle to the right-hand needle without knitting it
g	gram(s)			
in	inch(es)		**sl2**	slip two stitches from the left-hand needle to the right-hand needle without knitting them
inc	increase			
inc pwise	increase on a purl row		**ssk**	slip one stitch, slip one stitch, knit slipped stitches together
k	knit			
k2tog	knit two stitches together		**st(s)**	stitch(es)
kwise	knitwise		**st st**	stockinette (stocking) stitch
LH	left-hand		**tbl**	through back loop (work through the back loop of the stitch only)
m	meter(s)			
m1	make one stitch		**WS**	wrong side(s)
mm	millimeter		**yb**	yarn back, between the tips of the needles
oz	ounces		**yd**	yard(s)
p	purl		**yf**	yarn forward, between the tips of the needles
patt	pattern		**yo**	yarnover
p2tog	purl two stitches together		**[ ]**	work instructions within square brackets as directed
p3tog	purl three stitches together			
psso	pass slipped stitch over; pass a slipped stitch over another stitch		*****	work instructions after/between asterisk(s) as directed

suppliers

In case you need to top up your stash, here are some suggested yarn suppliers. For reasons of space we cannot cover all stockists, so please explore the local knitting shops and online stores in your own country.

USA

Love Crafts
Online sales
www.lovecrafts.com

Knitting Fever Inc.
www.knittingfever.com
Stockist locator on website

WEBS
Online sales
www.yarn.com

UK

Love Crafts
Online sales
www.lovecrafts.com

John Lewis
Retail stores and online
Tel: +44 (0)3456 049049
www.johnlewis.com
Telephone numbers of stores on website

Laughing Hens
Online store only
Tel: +44 (0)1829 740903
www.laughinghens.com

AUSTRALIA

Black Sheep Wool 'n' Wares
Retail store and online
Tel: +61 (0)2 6779 1196
www.blacksheepwool.com.au

Sun Spun Fine Yarns
Retail store only (Canterbury, Victoria)
Tel: +61 (0)3 9830 1609

index

author acknowledgments

Thanks to everyone who made this book possible, including Cindy Richards, Eliana Holder, Penny Craig, and Sally Powell from CICO Books, Marie Clayton my editor, photographers Caroline Arber and Terry Benson, stylists Nel Haynes, Sophie Martell, and Rob Merrett and illustrator Stephen Dew. Lastly, thanks to Roger, Louis and Louise—and my mum Paddy, whose twin sister Sheelagh first taught me how to knit.